DOROTHY
AND
WILLIAM WORDSWORTH

BY THE SAME AUTHOR

ALEXANDER SCOTT, MONTGOMERIE, AND
DRUMMOND OF HAWTHORNDEN
AS LYRIC POETS

DOROTHY
AND
WILLIAM WORDSWORTH

By

CATHERINE MACDONALD MACLEAN, M.A.

*Sometime Edmonstoune-Aytoun Fellow of the University
of Edinburgh; Lecturer in English in
University College, Cardiff*

HASKELL HOUSE PUBLISHERS Ltd.
Publishers of Scarce Scholarly Books
NEW YORK. N. Y. 10012
1972

HASKELL HOUSE PUBLISHERS LTD.

Publishers of Scarce Scholarly Books

280 LAFAYETTE STREET

NEW YORK. N. Y. 10012

Library of Congress Cataloging in Publication Data

Maclean, Catherine Macdonald.
  Dorothy and William Wordsworth.

  Reprint of the 1927 ed.
  1. Wordsworth, William, 1770-1850. 2. Wordsworth,
Dorothy, 1771-1855.
PR5881.M3 1972   821'.7 [B]   71-39678
ISBN 0-8383-1403-1

Printed in the United States of America

To

MY FATHER

PREFACE

I am indebted to Professor de Selincourt for permission to quote in these essays from his edition of *The Prelude*, and to Messrs Macmillan for permission to quote from *The Journals of Dorothy Wordsworth*.

I would wish to acknowledge gratefully the suggestion I have received from previous interpretations of Wordsworth's poetry, more especially those of M. Émile Legouis and of Professor Elton.

My thanks are due to Professor Grierson for his kindness in reading the proofs and in making suggestions, and to Professor Brett for a generous consideration but for which I should have had no leisure for writing.

C. M. M.

January 1927

ERRATUM

Page 107, line 7. *For* 1875 *read* 1888.

CONTENTS

I

A TOUR MADE IN SCOTLAND IN 1803

"Scotland is the country above all others that I have seen, in which a man of imagination may carve out his own pleasures."

DOROTHY WORDSWORTH

On August 22nd, 1803, a very tired horse drew through the outskirts of Glasgow a shabby Irish car, in which were seated two young men, somewhat dusty and travel-stained, and a slight, tanned, eager-faced girl, of a boyishness of appearance then most unfashionable. The quaintness of the "Hibernian vehicle" attracted more attention than quite suited the mood of the travellers, tired as they were after a day's journeying from Hamilton to Glasgow, and the children ceased their play to send a hooting after the strange equipage, so that the girl, who was looking round in a quick startled way, was glad when at length they reached the Saracen's Head. She writes: "I shall never forget how glad I was to be landed in a little quiet back-parlour, for my head was beating with the noise of carts which we had left, and the wearisomeness of the disagreeable objects near the highway;..."

It was not like these wayfarers, however, to be long fatigued or out of spirits. The following morning found them out of doors, and doing the sights of the city, although, confesses the girl, a renowned walker in her day, "I am less eager to walk in a large town than anywhere else;..." At 3 o'clock they left Glasgow, the

girl being now well muffled up in a serviceable grey
cloak to protect her from the heavy rain. It is she,
who, in giving an account of their departure, refutes for
ever the charge of lack of humour sometimes brought
against the citizens of Glasgow. "We were obliged
to ride through the streets to keep our feet dry," says
she, "and, in spite of the rain, every person as we went
along stayed his steps to look at us; indeed, we had the
pleasure of spreading smiles from one end of Glasgow
to the other—for we travelled the whole length of
the town."

The travellers, setting out light-heartedly for a
frugal jaunt through Scotland, were Dorothy and
William Wordsworth, who had left their cottage at
Grasmere on August 14th, and Coleridge, who had
joined them at Keswick on the 15th. Already they
had passed through Carlisle, and across the Solway
Moss into Scotland, through Dumfries, where Dorothy
pitied "poor Burns, and his moving about on that
unpoetic ground," through Leadhills and Lanark,
where Dorothy rejoiced in the beauty of the sunset.
"The evening sun was now sending a glorious light
through the street, which ran from west to east; the
houses were of a fire red, and the faces of the people
as they walked westward were almost like a black-
smith when he is at work by night." From Lanark
they passed to Hamilton. Their tour was to last six
weeks, and in the course of it they surveyed the greater
part of Scotland south of Inverness-shire. From
Glasgow they passed on to Dumbarton, and from

Dumbarton to Loch Lomond, Loch Katrine and the Trossachs. Thence, having been deserted by Coleridge, who probably found his eager companions too strenuous for him, they crossed to Inverary, and from Inverary they made their way to Glencoe. Turning eastwards, they visited Aberfeldy, Killiecrankie, Blair Atholl, Crieff and Callander, after which they paid a second visit to the magical Trossachs. On September 14th they were back at Callander. During the following days they visited Linlithgow, Edinburgh, Roslin (of Roslin chapel Dorothy gives an exquisite description), Hawthornden, Lasswade (where these tireless people visited Scott, arriving "before Mr and Mrs Scott had risen,") and Peebles. During the sixth week of their tour they visited Melrose (where Scott joined them), Dryburgh and Jedburgh. On September 22nd Scott, leaving his servant to drive his own gig, travelled with them in their car to Hawick, where he parted from them on the 23rd. On the 24th they were back again on known ground, half regretful that their spell of gipsying was at an end. The remainder of the journey must be given in Dorothy's own words: "Sunday, September 25th, 1803.—A beautiful autumnal day. Breakfasted at a public-house by the road-side; dined at Threlkeld; arrived at home between eight and nine o'clock, where we found Mary in perfect health, Joanna Hutchinson with her, and little John asleep in the clothes-basket by the fire."

The journal kept by Dorothy Wordsworth of this

tour is interesting first of all as recording the impression made on a woman of genius by the Scotland of 1803. It is a record, delicately clear, of a series of impressions made on a mind unusually sensitive and poetical, during a journey through a strange country which appealed peculiarly to the heart and the senses of the writer. In some ways it brings back to our minds that other most interesting record of travel, *A Journey to the Western Islands of Scotland.* Dorothy Wordsworth notes, as Johnson noted, the meanness of some of the inns, the poverty of many of the people, the desolation in the Highland glens owing to bad conditions and emigration, the simplicity of the food, the omnipresence of the dram. She writes of the ferryman's wife at Loch Katrine. "'She keeps a dram,' as the phrase is; indeed, I believe there is scarcely a lonely house by the wayside in Scotland where travellers may not be accommodated with a dram." Like Johnson too she notices the graciousness of Highland manners, and a hospitality carried to quixotry, sometimes even by the very poorest. But her gift is not, like Johnson's, for wise generalisation. Unlike Imlac she regards it as the business of the poet to "number the streaks of the tulip." Her gift is for detail, and through the delicate accuracy of her impressions, an accuracy which is no whit diminished because all these impressions are poetically conceived, she contrives to give the rhythm of the life of the country through which she is passing, sometimes the rhythm of life itself. She misses nothing in a land of

many contrasts. Scotland is shown to us through
a series of pictures. We see the little wild lads of
Wanlockhead, with honeysuckle on their hats, taking
to their heels when Coleridge questioned them on their
Latin—the English tourists at Lanark, who amused
Dorothy by setting out for Loch Lomond with the
pockets of their carriage stuffed with heather, "roots
and all"—the kind Highland woman exclaiming de-
lightedly, "Ho! yes, ye'll get that," every time Dorothy
stated one of her simple requirements—the boatman
who, although wet and cold, would not approach his
own fire until his guests had warmed themselves—the
Highland drovers in the inn at Inveroran "sitting in
a complete circle round a large peat-fire in the middle
of the floor, each with a mess of porridge, in a wooden
vessel, upon his knee"—the "joyous bustle" of the
boat-load of church-goers returning across Loch
Lomond, the men in tartan plaids and Scotch bonnets,
the women holding up green umbrellas to protect
their fine scarlet cloaks. And every now and again
something is described which affects the reader as
poetry itself—the sight of a shepherd lad, wrapped in
a grey plaid, alone with his sheep on the bare moor,
standing in utter quietness and silence—the beauty
of the fishermen's nets overshadowing the boats as
they were hung out to dry and "falling in the most
exquisitely graceful folds"—the meeting with the
solitary woman, begging by the banks of Loch Lomond,
"struggling with fatigue and poverty and unknown
ways"—the song of the boatman on Loch Lomond,

"a youth fresh from the Isle of Skye," who "could not speak a word of English, and sang a plaintive Gaelic air in a low tone while he plied his oar"—the utter peace of the shepherd, lying in the midst of a flock upon a sunny knoll, near the banks of the Tweed, with his face turned towards the sky—the solitary stone near Glenfalloch, which told of the people meeting to worship in the temple of the hills. At times, through one of these impressions, Dorothy gives a brief abstract and chronicle of the life of the "dwellers in the mist," as when she writes of the little herd lad near Tarbet.

While we were walking forward, the road leading us over the top of a brow, we stopped suddenly at the sound of a half-articulate Gaelic hooting from the field close to us. It came from a little boy, whom we could see on the hill between us and the lake, wrapped up in a grey plaid. He was probably calling home the cattle for the night. His appearance was in the highest degree moving to the imagination: mists were on the hill-sides, darkness shutting in upon the huge avenue of mountains, torrents roaring, no house in sight to which the child might belong; his dress, cry, and appearance all different from anything we had been accustomed to. It was a text...containing in itself the whole history of the Highlander's life—his melancholy, his simplicity, his poverty, his superstition, and above all, that visionariness which results from a communion with the unworldliness of nature.

In one respect Dorothy Wordsworth's journal differs greatly from Johnson's account. Johnson lent himself but grudgingly to the beauties of nature: to Dorothy Wordsworth the joy she received from watching the beauty of the world around her was half her life. It is impossible to overestimate the value of the descriptions she gives in her record. We can but marvel at the accuracy, the rigid truth, with which she records her impressions. It is this truth which makes each description have a life of its own, and linger in the memory as a beautiful thing. She is able to portray the very soul of places. There is no confusing the different beauties described in her pages. She finds the perfect words in which to describe the sweet serene beauty of the regions of the Tweed,

> More pensive in sunshine
> Than others in moonshine,

no less than to describe the mountains and the mists. There is something most delicately individual in her words. Of the Solway Moss she writes, "the dreary waste cheered by the endless singing of larks," and the words have the effect of an eagle's feather dropped on a moor. We never forget the place. She describes the Rock of Dumbarton in noble and simple prose. Her description of the little burying-ground on the banks of Loch Katrine lingers in the memory because of its deep peace, making even death seem companioned and companionable. The description of the view from Inch-ta-vannach, a view including "the ghostly image of Dumbarton Castle," and "so singular and beautiful that it was like a flash of images from another world," is one of the most intellectual of Dorothy's descriptions, intellectual because of the analysis it attempts of the nature of a beauty so magical and so enchanting.

She makes a brave attempt at describing the inde-
scribable beauty of a sunset sky, reflected "like melted
rubies" in the waters of a lake. She manages to give
an impression of Kilchurn Castle in a very few words,
"a decayed palace rising out of the plain of waters."
Of Mull, seen from the mainland, she writes, "...it was
of a gem-like colour, and as soft as the sky." She gives
up in despair the attempt to describe the mountains of
Glencoe, and then, through the leap of her imagination
to Milton, finds the very words. "They were such forms
as Milton might be supposed to have had in his mind
when he applied to Satan that sublime expression"—

His stature reached the sky.

In her description of Appin, as in that of the view
from Inch-ta-vannach, she attempts analysis.

I must say, however, that we hardly ever saw a thoroughly
pleasing place in Scotland, which had not something of
wildness in its aspect of one sort or other. It came from
many causes here: the sea, or sea-loch, of which we only
saw as it were a glimpse crossing the vale at the foot of it,
the high mountains on the opposite shore, the unenclosed
hills on each side of the vale, with black cattle feeding on
them, the simplicity of the scattered huts, the half-
sheltered, half-exposed situation of the village, the imperfect
culture of the fields, the distance from any city or large
town, and the very names of Morven and Appin, par-
ticularly at such a time, when Ossian's old friends, sun-
beams and mists, as like ghosts as any in the mid-afternoon
could be, were keeping company with them.

All these things were beautiful themselves. And
Dorothy Wordsworth succeeded in conveying an impression of their beauty, no small achievement. There

are times, however, when her prose is almost more
interesting than when she describes acknowledged
beauty and sublimity. These times are when she adds
something of her own personality to the thing seen,
when, as it were, she penetrates with her own beauty
of spirit, and illumines with her poetic fancy, things
which to the man who is neither a mystic nor a poet
would seem ordinary. In other words, she sheds over
commonplace objects the light of poetic imagination.
These are the rare moments of Dorothy Wordsworth,
and these are the moments which rendered her companionship so valuable to her brother, who recorded
these moments in verse. One such moment is that in
which Dorothy suddenly perceived the soft greeting,
"What, you are stepping westward?" as a gesture in
eternity. Another comes to her when looking at the
boat belonging to the house at the foot of Ben Dui-
rinnis. "The household boat lay at anchor, chained
to a rock, which, like the whole border of the lake, was
edged with sea-weed, and some fishing-nets were hung
upon poles,—affecting images, which led our thoughts
out to the wide ocean, yet made the solitudes of the
mountains bear the impression of greater safety and
more deep seclusion." An even more remarkable instance of Dorothy's apprehension of that beauty
which is itself poetry is given by her experience in the
inn parlour at Dumbarton, "dirty, and smelling of
liquors."

While tea was preparing we lolled at our ease, and though
the room-window overlooked the stable-yard, and at our

entrance there appeared to be nothing but gloom and un-loveliness, yet while I lay stretched upon the carriage cushion on three chairs, I discovered a little side peep which was enough to set the mind at work. It was no more than a smoky vessel lying at anchor, with its bare masts, a clay hut and the shelving bank of the river, with a green pasture above. Perhaps you will think that there is not much in this, as I describe it: it is true; but the effect produced by these simple objects, as they happened to be combined, together with the gloom of the evening, was exceedingly wild.

Constantly she receives this stimulus of beauty, which is the begetter of poetry.

It might seem as if a journal that was devoted mostly to description might be dull, but Dorothy Wordsworth is never dull. This is partly because her writing is so simple. Beautiful as is her prose, and touched with literary reminiscence, it is beautiful in an unpretentious way. It keeps near to life; and it is flexible. This being so, the writer is able at a moment's notice to pass from grave to gay, and from the sublime to the prosaic. The book is shot through with vivid and sometimes pungent character sketches. The descriptions of inns, and of landladies, sometimes are quite in the vein of Fielding, whom Dorothy knew well. Like *Joseph Andrews*, the journal might be named the Book of Inns. Here again, Dorothy's descriptions are individualised and make excellent reading. She gives many descriptions of the women with whom she had to deal. We do not forget the landlady at Leadhills, who found the climate "*varra halesome*," nor the ancient wraith of a woman, smoke-sodden from long

crouching over peat fires, who did the honours of
Dryburgh Abbey, nor the fat landlady at Luss, who
grudged the travellers a fire on a cold night, and who
drew from the charitable Dorothy one of the few un-
charitable comments she ever made: "She was over-
grown with fat, and was sitting with her feet and legs
in a tub of water for the dropsy,—probably brought on
by whisky drinking." The most vivid description of
all is that of the overworked woman of the King's
House, Glencoe, "screaming in Erse, with the most
horrible guinea-hen or peacock voice I ever heard,
first to one person, then another." This inn, where the
very horses stood like wild beasts, ready to devour
each other's portion of corn, remains in the memory
with the vividness of something seen in a fantastic
dream.

And Dorothy's stories too, told with an admirable
absence of comment, and charmingly natural and true,
punctuate the descriptions. "Among other questions
she asked me the old one over again, if I was married;
and when I told her that I was not, she appeared
surprised, and, as if recollecting herself, said to me,
with pious seriousness and perfect simplicity, 'To be
sure, there is a great promise for virgins in Heaven.'"

If it be not too fantastic to compare the book with
Joseph Andrews, the Parson Adams (in so far as he is
the victim of the entertainment) is perhaps the poor
horse, whose chief troubles, however, arose from the
fact that he did not share the joyous indifference of
Parson Adams to wading through streams. The

troubles of this unfortunate horse began at an early stage of the journey, but reached a climax at Connel Ferry, which left him with an unconquerable prejudice against water, in a country where the streams are innumerable. Near Glencoe he gave unmistakable signs that mountain scenery was distasteful to him, and from that time onward was liable to "*crises de nerfs*" at the most awkward moments. There are times when we censure the heartlessness of the heroines of romance, who are apt to discard their palfreys when they have no further use for them, but no one could have blamed Dorothy if she had left this joyless animal, who entered so little into the spirit of the enterprise, to wander for ever on the far side of the Tweed, even as the more deserving horse of Parthenopeus was left whinnying on the sea shore.

Perhaps the best thing that this journal gives altogether is not the description of Scotland, almost three decades after Johnson visited it, interesting as that description is, nor even its poetic flashes, nor its noble and simple prose, nor its gaiety, nor its remarkable character sketches, but the impression we get from it of a rare and exquisite spirit, pursuing its exquisite ways. Most journals are introspective. This journal always looks outward. Yet we get from it the impression of a woman, brave, tender, resourceful, vital, rich in the capacity for enjoyment, unselfish, uncomplaining as a starved kitten waiting on a doorstep until someone chance to open the door, patient, enduring, humorous, and most innocent. And she

is simple as a child, and gay with a child's eager gaiety.
It is entirely characteristic of this woman that the
most beautiful of all her pictures (and one showing
very remarkably her power of transfiguration) is the
picture of a ferryman's hut, as it seemed to her after
a long cold day outside. It reveals much, too, of the
ardour of the Wordsworths and of Coleridge in their
young days, and it is as fantastic as it is simple:

It was dark when we landed, and on entering the house
I was sick with cold.

The good woman had provided, according to her promise,
a better fire than we had found in the morning; and indeed
when I sate down in the chimney-corner of her smoky
biggin' I thought I had never been more comfortable in my
life. Coleridge had been there long enough to have a pan
of coffee boiling for us, and having put our clothes in the
way of drying, we all sate down, thankful for a shelter....

We caroused our cups of coffee, laughing like children at
the strange atmosphere in which we were: the smoke came
in gusts, and spread along the walls and above our heads
in the chimney, where the hens were roosting like light
clouds in the sky. We laughed and laughed again, in spite
of the smarting of our eyes, yet had a quieter pleasure in
observing the beauty of the beams and rafters gleaming
between the clouds of smoke. They had been crusted over
and varnished by many winters, till, where the firelight fell
upon them, they were as glossy as black rocks on a sunny
day cased in ice....

I went to bed some time before the family. The door was
shut between us, and they had a bright fire, which I could
not see; but the light it sent up among the varnished
rafters and beams, which crossed each other in almost as
intricate and fantastic a manner as I have seen the under-
boughs of a large beech-tree withered by the depth of the
shade above, produced the most beautiful effect that can

be conceived. It was like what I should suppose an underground cave or temple to be, with dripping or moist roof, and the moonlight entering in upon it by some means or other, and yet the colours were more like melted gems. I lay looking up till the light of the fire faded away, and the man and his wife and child had crept into their bed at the other end of the room. I did not sleep much, but passed a comfortable night, for my bed, though hard, was warm and clean: the unusualness of my situation prevented me from sleeping. I could hear the waves beat against the shores of the lake; a little "syke" close to the door made a much louder noise; and when I sate up in my bed I could see the lake through an open window-place at the bed's head. Add to this, it rained all night. I was less occupied by the remembrance of the Trossachs, beautiful as they were, than the vision of the Highland hut, which I could not get out of my head. I thought of the Fairyland of Spenser....

But the woman who could write thus of a three-roomed Highland cottage had no need of Spenser's Fairyland. She had the key to a Fairyland of her own, which she could enter at any moment. It is because she could open this door to her brother the poet, that the bond which united Dorothy and William Wordsworth was so passionate and so enduring.

II
DOROTHY WORDSWORTH

DOROTHY WORDSWORTH

"...it made me more than half a poet."
                                    Grasmere journal

These words break in on the enchantment of that record of ardent days given by Dorothy Wordsworth's Grasmere journal. The modesty of the estimate, coming as it does from the most poetical woman of her generation at the close of one of those passages that take the breath with their beauty, shocks the reader. But it was entirely characteristic of the writer. Never was there a less self-conscious woman than Dorothy Wordsworth, nor a less pretentious one.

This utter absence of any claim to literary merit obscured somewhat the fame of Dorothy Wordsworth for her own generation. This is not to say that she was not valued. Every now and then contemporary men of letters paid tribute to her rare gift. Yet the appreciation given to her work seems but faint, when we remember that she was the most remarkable writer of prose in a generation that included De Quincey. De Quincey himself is to some extent affected in his estimate by the memory of Dorothy's entire lack of assumption. It is strange to find him, after paying tribute to an art at once stronger and more delicate than his own, concluding with the words, "To talk of her 'writings' is too pompous an expression, or at least far beyond any pretensions that she ever made for herself."

2-2

The fame of Dorothy Wordsworth has never recovered from this estimate. She has not lacked her sworn admirers (Mark Rutherford was one of them), but she has never taken her rightful place in the republic of letters. It is difficult even now to make as close an acquaintance as could be wished with the work of this lady "of Egyptian brown." We have no complete edition either of her letters or of her journals, and we have no full and accurate biography. We still have to judge of her from partial records.

She was born in Cockermouth on December 25th, 1771. Her mother died in 1778. Such glimpses as we get of her in her earliest days are from the conversations of Wordsworth and Dorothy, and from the poems. Wordsworth gives one or two delightful impressions of the "little Prattler among men." For nine years after her mother's death she lived chiefly at Halifax under the care of her mother's cousin, Miss Threlkeld. During these years her great friend was Jane Pollard, with whom she walked and talked and ran wild and dreamed dreams. At Halifax she was very happy. It was not until she went to live with her grandparents at Penrith in 1787 that Dorothy felt homeless. Her letters show how galling for a time became her dependence on conventional and unsympathetic relatives. More galling still to her was the ungenerous treatment given to those brothers of whom she was so proud, and the subjection of "William" to petty tyrannies. Her letters make us understand the austerities that the Wordsworths were afterwards ready to endure for independence, the economies which sometimes meant positive hardship. The girl of fifteen —enduring not only a spiritual isolation which was the hardest of all things for her to bear, but such petty humiliations as could only come to one left to the mercy of others—felt that sense of cramping and oppression which, once suffered in youth, leaves ever afterwards a proud and eager independence.

In December 1788 she went to live with an uncle at Forncett, remaining with him until December 1793. Her life, during this period, seems to centre in her brother. His brief visits were pleasures to be relived in the imagination. She writes to Miss Pollard.

It was in winter (at Christmas) that he was last at Forn-cett; and every day, as soon as we rose from dinner, we used to pace the gravel walk in the garden till six o'clock, when we received a summons (which was always welcome) to tea. Nothing but rain or snow prevented our taking this walk. Often have I gone out, when the keenest north wind has been whistling amongst the trees over our heads, and have paced that walk in the garden, which will always be dear to me—from the remembrance of those very long conversations I have had upon it supported by my brother's arm. Ah! I never thought of the cold when he was with me.

Already her letters begin to show some of the quality which makes her journals so distinctive.

During 1794 she was partly in Halifax, partly wandering with William. How free and joyous are her descriptions of her life with him at the farm of Windy Brow. "We please ourselves in calculating from our present expenses for how very small a sum we could

live. We find our own food. Our breakfast and supper
are of milk, and our dinner chiefly of potatoes, and
we drink no tea." "And we drink no tea." What a
gesture of emancipation there is in that phrase! And
what a proud (albeit entirely civil) letter of defiance
Dorothy writes to her Aunt Crackanthorpe, who dis-
approves of her unconventional mode of life, and of
all this gipsying with a restless brother.

The gipsying came to an end all too quickly, but in
September 1795 Dorothy and William set up house at
Racedown. A legacy of £900, bequeathed to William
by Raisley Calvert, gave promise of greater security
of fortune than they had hitherto enjoyed. The years
that followed were Dorothy's golden years, and de-
spite the slenderness of their joint resources, the brother
and sister attained almost perfect happiness. In March
1797 Dorothy writes to her friend, "The dreams of our
ardent imaginations have not proved shadowy." In
the spring of 1797 they first entertained Coleridge at
Racedown. In July of that year, attracted by the
magnetism of Coleridge, who was living at Nether
Stowey, they lightheartedly transferred themselves to
Alfoxden. We are rich in knowledge of their life at
that time. Hazlitt has left impressions of it. Dorothy
herself began to record the happiness of each day in the
delicate fine prose of her journal. It is perhaps from
Cottle, a spectator of this life, that we get the sharpest
impression of it as it appeared to an outsider, extraordinarily care-free, joyous, simple, even primitive.

The brother and sister spent this year in the seventh

heaven of creative rapture. After the publication of the *Lyrical Ballads* Dorothy spent a winter with William in Germany. At the end of 1799 she settled with him in Dove Cottage, Grasmere. From this time onwards, the records of her life, identified as it was with Wordsworth's, are very full. She had many friends, and she wrote many letters. Her letters give us the fullest impression we have, not only of the Wordsworth, but of the Coleridge household, and of Coleridge himself, in the fullness of his power, and in his deterioration. The early letters tell of the eager happiness of the years when she was all in all to William. The later ones show her after Wordsworth's marriage in 1802, resolutely turning away from any repining, and entering not only into the big joys and sorrows of the growing family, but into every pleasure and every vexation. When workmen are tiresome and chimneys smoke, Dorothy's letters are all of workmen and smoky chimneys. It is from her that we get most of our impressions of Wordsworth's family—of "Johnny with his shamefaced smile" and knack of making fairy tales for himself—of Dora, beautiful and wayward— of Thomas the innocent and blue eyed, whose death left her with such an aching sense of loss—of little plain humorous Catherine whom she loved so well. It is from her we know that Wordsworth could be whimsical.

Her letters are surely the most selfless letters that ever were written. She is always quite free from thought of herself. Discomfort finds her uncomplaining, and when the habit of economy, always strong on her,

makes her prefer to endure hardship rather than to
pay for comfort, she has the knack of turning her
hardships into rare and valuable experiences, as when
she writes to Lady Beaumont in August 1810, making
light of a cold night journey on the outside of a coach.

Throughout these busy years, much of her scanty
leisure was given to walking, in which she took in-
creasing pleasure. She seems to become more and
more thankful for it. As late as 1828, we find her
planning once more to ascend Helvellyn. In 1829, a
complete breakdown put an end to walking and to all
other activities. The immediate reasons of this illness
were exhaustion and exposure during a long walk. But
we cannot help feeling that other remote things
played their part in it, and that her strength had been
overtaxed for years. The austerities of her youth, the
passionate ardour of her life with her brother between
1795 and 1802 (there is no doubt at all that she lived
too hard during these years)—the brave voiceless
surrender of her joy in 1802, at the time of Wordsworth's marriage—the wear and tear of the bringing
up of the Wordsworth family—the constant drain im-
posed on her strength by the fervour of her spirit—the
sapping of her vitality by that extraordinary capacity
for sympathy (constituting half her charm) which
De Quincey noted—all these no doubt contributed to
her breakdown.

She expected her illness to be transitory, and fought
against the suggestion of invalidism. But she was
fighting against forces beyond her control. In 1836

Mary Wordsworth writes describing Dorothy's painful
and uncontrollable emotion on being brought out to
the garden. But it is evident that by this time Mary
is bewildered. A touch of wild gaiety, and a touch of
perverseness in Dorothy, baffled her. Dorothy's suf-
ferings had passed beyond Mrs Wordsworth's ken,
good and kind as she was; and they had sapped both
mind and body. It is Dorothy herself, in a letter of
1837, who comes nearest to explaining them. She'
writes: "A madman might as well attempt to relate
the history of his own doings, and those of his fellows
in confinement, as I to tell you one hundredth part of
what I have felt, suffered, and done."

There is something unbearably sad about the last
twenty-six years of her life, during which her broken
spirit lingered pitiably in her broken body. With the
death of her brother in 1850, the last flicker of light
went out for her. She died in 1855.

We turn away from the contemplation of these sad
inexplicable years to those writings in which her
eager and innocent spirit found enduring expression.
Throughout a very busy life she experienced a constant
urge to write. Yet she is not quite a woman of letters.
Books did not come first with her, and she read purely
where her fancy roved. This waywardness of hers,
conjoined as it was to brilliant critical powers, half
annoyed De Quincey. But it is just this waywardness
which makes her criticism so interesting. Dorothy's
taste from the beginning was very delicate and very

sure. Even to William's early work she will not give
undue praise. Coleridge from the beginning realised
the delicacy of her taste. Yet Dorothy never professed
to be a critic. And just as she stumbled into criticism,
she stumbled into art, urged in the first instance by
the necessity of giving expression to the sheer beauty
and poignancy of those few brief years in which her
happiness had been exquisite. She was not deliberately
creative, and all her work consists of her journals. Her
first journal was begun at Alfoxden in January 1798,
and continued until May. The second was written in
Hamburg, later in that year. While at Grasmere she
kept a record intermittently between May 1800 and
January 1803. From this time, the intimate record
drops. But at intervals during her life Dorothy kept
journals of her wanderings. She wrote a long journal
of the tour she made with her brother in Scotland in
1803, a journal of a mountain ramble in 1805, a
journal of a tour on the continent in 1820, and a
second journal of a tour in Scotland in 1822. Her last
journal, written in 1828, was on a tour in the Isle of
Man.

In these journals that are so much more than
journals Dorothy shows herself the greatest of English
descriptive writers. Her art gives itself triumphantly
to analysis. Her descriptions owe something of their
character to their birth. A good deal of their beauty is
based on their rigid accuracy of observation and of
colouring. The accuracy in itself delights. We would
rejoice in it, even if it were not made contributory to

beauty. Dorothy notices all sorts of little things. She notes that the heads of the snowdrops are "at first upright, ribbed with green," but afterwards droop; that the birch trees are "of a bright red, through which gleams a shade of purple"; that the brooms, covered with snow, are like "arched feathers with wiry stalks pointed to the end, smaller and smaller." Her descriptions are full of interesting detail. Even when she observes the ravens high in the sky, she must pause to notice the whiteness of their bellies in the sunshine.

The descriptions owe something to the eager life that pulsates in them. All she describes seems to take on life. This is partly because she lives with the things she describes, so that they become real to her, and she respects their life. Gravely she replants the uprooted strawberry blossom. "It will have but a stormy life of it, but let it live if it can." The mists and the shadows become as living companions to her. There are times when the shadows seem to her more like living things than the birds that cause them. Some of her loveliest descriptions are of these shifting things, mists and shadows and the strange effects of light that suddenly array the workaday world in gem-like splendour.

What does more than any other one thing to give the journals their specific quality, is the keenness of the writer's perception of beauty. She has the spirit of the true pastoral poet. "Earth and sky were so lovely that they melted our very hearts," she exclaims. This perception, always keen, is quickened in the Grasmere journals by the sharpness of the emotional crisis through which Dorothy Wordsworth, preparing to welcome William Wordsworth's wife, was passing. Her observation is that of a woman whose senses have all been sharpened because she is in the grip of great emotion. It is not too much to say that she writes in a state of exaltation, and that the reader sees all that she sees coloured through this exaltation. She adds strangeness and sweetness to all that she describes. She writes: "As I lay down on the grass, I observed the glittering silver line on the ridge of the backs of the sheep, owing to their situation respecting the sun, which made them look beautiful, but with something of strangeness, like animals of another kind, as if belonging to a more splendid world.... "

There is transfiguration in this description. She has the poet's vision.

She has too, the poet's ear, which hears the music of the universe, that music which uncle Gottfried captured for little Jean-Christophe to hear*. As Jean-Christophe listened when his uncle bade him, we listen to Dorothy, and as we listen, all sorts of slender pipings form themselves into a symphony. We catch something of this music when she writes: "The shutters were closed, but I heard the birds singing. There was our own thrush, shouting with an impatient shout; so it sounded to me. The morning was still, the twittering of the little birds was very gloomy. The owls had hooted a quarter of an hour before, now the cocks were

* Romain Rolland, *Jean-Christophe*, 1.

crowing, it was near daylight, I put out my candle, and went to bed." It sounds for us in the description of the swallows singing their little twittering song over their fallen nest. It sounds for us in her description of the last night at Grasmere before Wordsworth brought Mary Hutchinson to it as his bride. "I read the *Winter's Tale*; then I went to bed, but did not sleep. The swallows stole in and out of their nest, and sate there, *whiles* quite still, *whiles* they sung low for two minutes or more, at a time just like a muffled robin."

It is inevitable that description of this kind should tend ultimately to the criticism and description of life itself. Gradually a picture of life takes shape from the journals of Dorothy Wordsworth. We value in the early journals the picture of a Westmorland Arcadia that is not all Arcadia, the pictures of Scotland and of the continent in the later ones. In the presentation of this life once more we admire the simplicity and the perfect naturalness of the writing, a naturalness that allows of the easy transition from the prosaic and the trivial to a beauty and sweetness that are deeply moving. They are like the Icelandic sagas in the way in which a record of the trivial details of life in the dales suddenly merges into great beauty. The writing is as natural and unforced as the singing of larks. But there are deep notes too. One thing that prevents it from being merely a record, and that co-relates it to the great things of literature, is the presence of a deep pity. A sense of pity is constant in

Dorothy Wordsworth's writing; and the sorrowful
underworld, too, has its "authentic comment." In the
dales of Westmorland the serenity of the dalesman
is broken by ugly stories from the outside world, and
we meet in these dales the uncomplaining hungry
child going to "late a lock" of meal, just as we meet
by the banks of Loch Lomond the solitary beggar
woman, and in Calais the "squalid, ragged woman" to
whom Dorothy gave a penny with an effect "almost
as of something supernatural."

For describing all this material, Dorothy Wordsworth found the perfect words. Even judged by the
severest test of all, the test of the single word, she is
triumphant. Her words have individuality from the
beginning. Her girlish letters have a stateliness as well
as a simplicity of phrase, marking at once a mag-
nanimity as well as a delicacy of mind. This distinction
of phrase is natural and effortless. "How we are squan-
dered abroad..." is her comment on the dispersal
of herself and her brothers. "I cannot foresee the day
of my felicity, the day on which I am once more to
find a home under the same roof as my brother. All·
is still obscure and dark." she writes in 1793. In the
account of the Patterdale walk, she finds the exact
words in which to describe the "small rain." She
writes: "...there was never a drop upon my habit larger
than the smallest pearls upon a lady's ring." Again,
in words as perfect as they are simple she writes: "The
moonlight lay upon the hills like snow." William felt
this haunting turn of phrase. At the close of 1799,

describing the "third waterfall" which Dorothy and he
viewed on their journey from Sockburn to Grasmere,
he quotes her words admiringly*. "After cautiously
sounding our way over stones of all colours and sizes,
encased in the clearest water formed by the spray of
the fall, we found the rock, which before had appeared
like a wall, extending itself over our heads, like the
ceiling of a huge cave, from the summit of which the
waters shot directly over our heads into a bason, and
among fragments wrinkled over with masses of ice as
white as snow, or rather, as Dorothy says, like con-
gealed froth." Sometimes he could not get away from
her perfection of phrase. He was faced with the problem of down-right plagiarism, or with the necessity
of making use of words less true: We know very well
what has happened to William when we read: "After
tea I read to William that account of the little boy
belonging to the tall woman, and an unlucky thing it
was, for he could not escape from those very words,
and so he could not write the poem. He left it un-
finished and went tired to bed."

The unconscious humour of this account of William,
unable to write his poem because of the tiresome inevitability of Dorothy's phrasing, is hard to beat.

There is never any dimming of the lustre in Dorothy
Wordsworth's writing. Unlike her more famous
brother, she was a poet at heart to the end, and shaken
by the poet's dangerous ecstasy. And she is never
falsely poetical, because, being content with sim-

* C. Wordsworth, *Memoirs*, i, pp. 152-3.

plicities, she never seeks to soar. If she has the faculty
of making us see the world in a grain of sand, that is
because she has the poet's heart, not because she is
striving after effect. Neither in the *Journal of a Tour
on the Continent* nor in her last journal of 1828 is there
any suggestion of diminishing power. Indeed, it is
the keenness of feeling in the journal of 1820 that is
somewhat troubling, for it must have been wearing
to any spirit. There lives within the "very flame" of
such feeling "a kind of wick or snuff that will abate
it." A note of danger sounds in the words: "While
I lay on my bed, the terrible solitudes of the Wetterhorn were revealed by fits—its black chasms, and snowy,
dark, grey summits. All night, and all day, and for
ever, the vale of Meiringen is sounding with torrents."
We note too, in this journal, dim intimations of sadness.

Such intimations of sadness as Dorothy Wordsworth
gave were ever dim. We can only guess, from stray
words and gestures, of her deepest longings. It is only
a chance word from William which lets us know that
during her long decline her imprisoned thoughts were
with the days before she came to Grasmere, when "all
the world was fresh and new." And when we read of
her delight in the robin who took up his abode in her
room and companioned her in 1835, we have to turn
to the early journal of 1798 and the many descriptions
of the robins singing in the leafless boughs, to realise
that her thoughts had gone back to the woods of
Alfoxden, and the "slender notes" which from day to
day she had not disdained to chronicle.

III

DOROTHY AND WILLIAM WORDSWORTH

DOROTHY AND WILLIAM WORDSWORTH

"...Oh! these poets!...They have such pens! and such
ink! and never a pen-knife!"

DOROTHY WORDSWORTH to MRS CLARKSON

There is occasionally a tendency, on the part of admirers of Dorothy Wordsworth, to look upon Wordsworth as "the villain in the piece." This attitude is
foreshadowed in the faint irritation showed by Samuel
Rogers over his meeting with the Wordsworths in
Scotland in 1803.

During our excursion we fell in with Wordsworth, Miss
Wordsworth, and Coleridge, who were, at the same time,
making a tour in a vehicle that looked very like a cart.
Wordsworth and Coleridge were entirely occupied in talking
about poetry; and the whole care of looking out for cottages where they might get refreshment and pass the night,
as well as seeing their poor horse fed and littered, devolved
upon Miss Wordsworth. She was a most delightful person,
—so full of talent, so simple-minded and so modest! *

There is a stronger irritation shown by a present-
day critic over Wordsworth's characterisation of his
sister's emotion after saying good-bye to Coleridge as
"nervous blubbering." And indeed it cannot be
claimed that the phrase shows any excess of sympathy.

It is the purpose of this essay to comment upon
such an attitude.

There can be no doubt that Wordsworth was indebted to his sister in an extraordinary degree. As a
girl, she gave him love and belief; as a woman, she gave

* *Recollections of the Table Talk of Samuel Rogers*, p. 208.

3-2

him love and belief, and unquenchable sympathy and unstinted service. She shielded him from household worries, and relieved him of any drudgery that might hamper his flight. She was to him such a companion as few men have ever had. She walked with him when he wished to walk, talked with him when he wished to talk, kept silence when the mood of silence was on him, did the mending and the ironing and the baking when he wished to write, soothed him when he was weary or unsuccessful, played with him when he wished to play, wrote his letters and mended the poet's troublesome pens. More than all this, she gave him his poetic baptism. So much did she do for him, that we are tempted to round off our sense of Wordsworth's indebtedness to her by saying: "She told Wordsworth that he was a poet, and proceeded to make him one."

Even as we say this, we know that we have fallen a prey to the idol of partisanship. We have exaggerated a debt, in the attempt to receive some acknowledgment of its existence. Wordsworth did not require Dorothy to make him a poet. The well of poetry is pure and deep. There was in him a well of poetry which not even Dorothy could touch. Before his association with her had been close he had had the poet's vision, and had felt the poet's trouble.

> ...after I had seen
> That spectacle, for many days, my brain
> Work'd with a dim and undetermined sense
> Of unknown modes of being; in my thoughts
> There was a darkness, call it solitude,
> Or blank desertion, no familiar shapes

> Of hourly objects, images of trees,
> Of sea or sky, no colours of green fields;
> But huge and mighty Forms that do not live
> Like living men mov'd slowly through the mind
> By day and were the trouble of my dreams.

And after close association with her, these experiences of his remained the same. Dorothy's journal of 1801 gives a curious testimony as to the continuance of these hauntings. She writes:

> William went to John's Grove. I went to find him. Moonlight, but it rained....He had been surprised and terrified by a sudden rushing of winds, which seemed to bring earth sky and lake together, as if the whole were going to enclose him in. He was glad he was in a high road.

The exaltation which Wordsworth got from Nature was something which he shared with no other. He had from the beginning a touch almost of religious awe, as is shown by the fine letter which he wrote to his sister from Switzerland in 1790. And he had a message to deliver. In both these respects he differed from his sister. Dorothy did not have these shattering semi-mystical experiences. It was the sheer beauty of the world about her that drove her to describe. It is perhaps just this, that she was content to paint, and did not desire to preach, which makes her work dear to many to-day who have ceased to find healing in Wordsworth. She "calls home the heart to quietness."

What was deepest in Wordsworth's poetry was his own. It is something which will be found in Wordsworth, and in no other writer, not even in Dorothy. For this, Wordsworth would doubtless have found expression even if he had not come under Dorothy's influence. And the fragment of *The Recluse* makes it clear to us that he knew this possession to be his, and his alone. But this constitutes only the inner core of Wordsworth's poetry, a stubborn hard core that nothing would ever have altered.

For all the rest, he was enormously indebted to his sister. "She gave me eyes, she gave me ears;" said the poet, and it was literally the truth. She taught him to hear the "low and wren-like warblings" and "slender notes," which his ear would otherwise have missed. While the deepest strain in Wordsworth's poetry came from the poet himself, the poems expressive of this strain by no means constitute the bulk of his poetry. And for the remainder he was indebted to Dorothy. She, too, had a poet's vision. She described to Wordsworth what she saw. And her vision, as well as his own, he incorporated in his poetry.

Three gifts Dorothy had—the gift of observation, the gift of receiving those impressions which become the substance of poetry, and the gift of getting into touch with all sorts of people and of envisaging their lives. And each of these gifts went to enrich Wordsworth's poetry. She was the source of constant inspiration. The only proof of this that is needed is a comparison of Wordsworth's poems with Dorothy's journals.

Wordsworth dealt with all this wonderful material, with very varying degrees of success. His handling of it does not always satisfy. On January 25th, 1798, Dorothy writes:

Went to Poole's after tea. The sky spread over with one continuous cloud, whitened by the light of the moon, which, though her dim shape was seen, did not throw forth so strong a light as to chequer the earth with shadows. At once the clouds seemed to cleave asunder, and left her in the centre of a black-blue vault. She sailed along, followed by multitudes of stars, small, and bright, and sharp.

The description is beautifully clear. *A Night Piece*, which describes the same sky, is like a faint copy, and it has failed to capture the clear beauty which Dorothy's words convey. On March 1st, 1798, Dorothy writes: "The shapes of the mist, slowly moving along, exquisitely beautiful; passing over the sheep they almost seemed to have more of life than these quiet creatures. The unseen birds singing in the mist." This note has more of poetry in it than any of the verses Wordsworth wrote about this time. On March 10th she writes: "... interesting groups of human creatures, the young frisking and dancing in the sun, the elder quietly drinking in the life and soul of the sun and air." This is the prose equivalent of Wordsworth's poem on "the spirit of the season."

On March 18th she describes a parting with the Coleridges: "The Coleridges left us. A cold, windy morning. Walked with them half way. On our return sheltered under the hollies, during a hail-shower. The withered leaves danced with the hailstones." We cannot feel

that William improves upon this simple description
when he writes:

> But see! where'er the hailstones drop
> The withered leaves all skip and hop,

On April 17th, 1802, she writes: "I saw a robin chasing
a scarlet butterfly this morning." On the 18th William
wrote *The Robin and the Butterfly*, a poem in which the
vividness that Dorothy calls up is lost. Occasionally
he seizes upon an incident that has already been
perfectly expressed, and expresses it in a form that is
just a trifle too heavy for the gossamer beauty of the
impression which the sensitive Dorothy has caught.
Her description of the beautiful Highland girl at Loch
Lomond is all that is needed. "One of the girls was
exceedingly beautiful; and the figures of both of them,
in grey plaids falling to their feet, their faces only being
uncovered, excited our attention before we spoke to
them;"

This rings truer than the lines,

> Sweet Highland Girl, a very shower
> Of beauty is thy earthly dower!
> Twice seven consenting years have shed
> Their utmost bounty on thy head:

and Dorothy's description of the greeting, "What,
you are stepping westward?" is perfect. She says:
"I cannot describe how affecting this simple expression
was in that remote place, with the western sky in front,
yet glowing with the departed sun." We need no more.
We know just what Dorothy felt. Wordsworth's
verses, written some time after, somewhat labour

the delicate beauty. It is as if he had caught a butterfly.

Often he handles his material more skilfully; and gives a pleasurable account in verse of something of which Dorothy had already given a pleasurable account in prose. Dorothy's description of the daffodils, and Wordsworth's verses, are both delightful. Sometimes the leaven of her words worked in him after a long time. On March 13th, 1802, she writes: "William finished *Alice Fell*, and then wrote the poem of *The Beggar Woman*, taken from a woman whom I had seen in May (now nearly two years ago)...." At other times he caught fire immediately.

There are times when Wordsworth transcends his sister and sublimates an impression of the kind she was wont to receive. This happens in *The Leech Gatherer*, which cost Wordsworth much effort, and Dorothy much solicitude in consequence.

Dorothy gave Wordsworth a great deal. She gave him all she had to give, except her quick sense of humour. Yet, as we read her journals, our wonder is, not that he took so much, but that he did not take more. They are so rich in the rough material of poetry. Much of them consists of poetry, unwrought into verse. One thing is worth noticing, that as Wordsworth's faculty decayed, he ceased to receive inspiration even from Dorothy, who retained her powers as long as she wrote. "You certainly have the gift of setting him on fire." she wrote to Crabb Robinson in 1822. This remark, with its generous assumption that "old Crabb" could begin where she had ended, is quite beyond comment. Her journal of 1820, like the record of Scottish travel in 1803, contains a succession of beautiful descriptions. Her exactitude can find no colour to describe "the small pyramids" around a glacier but "of a greyish colour, mingled with vitriol green." She finds the only words in which to describe the Fall of the Reichenbach, "What weight and speed of waters! And what a tossing of grey mist!"—to describe the waters of the Rhine falling "like liquid emeralds"—to describe "the terrible solitudes" of the Alps. Her phrasing is gracious as ever. We pause now and again to savour the beauty of her words, as when she writes of the "grey adamantine towers," of the Wetterhorn, or, "Mont Blanc...lifting his resplendent forehead above a vapoury sea." She retains unimpaired her gift of conveying to the reader what is new and picturesque in a strange country, through presenting a number of impressions. Of Belgium she writes: "The fondness for flowers appears in this country wherever you go. Nothing is more common than to see a man, driving a cart, with a rose in his mouth. At the very top of our ascent I saw one at work with his spade, a full-blown rose covering his lips..."

Yet all this freshness, all this vividness, all this beauty failed to rouse Wordsworth, whose verses on this tour are flat and stale.

To suggest that Wordsworth was guilty of anything like plagiarism is nonsense. His specific gift is quite different from Dorothy's. She is made no whit the poorer by her brother's gain, and by the suggestions he caught from her richness. The fact was, these two had the knack of setting each other on fire. If any criticism is to be made on Wordsworth's use of Dorothy's material, it is that he did not seem to realise the beauty of that on which he drew. This is suggested by his cavalier treatment of the Patterdale tour of 1805, which he included, altered so as to obscure its charm somewhat, in his *Guide through the District of the Lakes*; by his neglecting to publish the excellent record of travel in Scotland, and by his failure to make any distinction between the records of travel on the continent kept by his wife and those by his sister. These things leave little doubt that he did not realise that the material he was borrowing from Dorothy and fashioning into new shapes was already gold. With this obtuseness of his with regard to a poetic inspiration more constant than his own, it is impossible not to feel the utmost impatience. There is only one excuse for him. Dorothy's extraordinary modesty might have misled even a surer critic than William Wordsworth.

Apart from his failure to estimate the value of her work and the rare character of her talent (a talent which others were quick to perceive and to value), Wordsworth made to Dorothy the fullest repayment it was possible for a man with his nature to make. He put himself first, for his nature was egoistical, just as Dorothy put herself last, because her nature was self-less. But he loved her in the measure which his egoism

allowed. In giving her a home, he gave her the fulfil-
ment of her day-dreams. In giving her himself to
guard against the irritating interruptions of ordinary
responsibilities, he satisfied the deepest need of her
generous nature. In acknowledgment of his intellectual debt, he placed her along with Coleridge, a
grand acknowledgment. And he was always ample
in acknowledgment of the miracle of her personality.
His poems are strewn with testimonies of her graciousness. He writes:

> Her voice was like a hidden Bird that sang,
> The thought of her was like a flash of light,
> Or an unseen companionship, a breath
> Of fragrance independent of the Wind.

His words begin to soar when he writes of her. He
begins one of his poems on her with the line "Among
all lovely things my Love had been." He writes of
her as

> ...She who dwells with me, whom I have loved
> With such communion, that no place on earth
> Can ever be a solitude to me,

and he wrote for her the lovely sheaf of Lucy poems,
full of a deep quiet love.

Even if Wordsworth had not thus repaid his sister's
devotion, Dorothy would have been amply rewarded.
Such love as hers is its own reward. Through her union
with Wordsworth she touched ecstasy. The years she
had with him, from 1795 to 1802, were the years which
for her justified the adventure of living. After 1802
it was perhaps inevitable, that as Wordsworth's life

grew richer, hers should grow poorer. Nothing ever made up to her for the loss of the enchanted days. She never complained. But there are shadowy suggestions of a habit of suffering in the 1820 journal. Of the days of enchantment, however, she could never be dispossessed. The Grasmere journals speak of them unforgettably. They make stirring reading, these records of an intimate companionship, to which one hardly dare apply the name passionate lest the nature of its enchantment should be misunderstood. The brother and sister lived intensely. With the departure of William even for a few days, the world seemed to stop for Dorothy. Every question that delays her from reading his letters is "like the snapping of a little thread" about her heart. The intensity of their affection may be read in the following record of an afternoon's companionship.

I went and sate with W. and walked backwards and forwards in the orchard till dinner-time. He read me his poem. I read to him, and my Beloved slept. A sweet evening as it had been a sweet day, and I walked quietly along the side of Rydale lake with quiet thoughts—the hills and the lake were still—the owls had not begun to hoot, and the little birds had given over singing. I looked before me and saw a red light upon Silver How as if coming out of the vale below,

"There was a light of most strange birth,
A light that came out of the earth,
And spread along the dark hill-side."

Thus I was going on when I saw the shape of my Beloved in the road at a little distance. We turned back to see the light but it was fading—almost gone.

The companionship is so perfect that at times it seems to border the deeps where pain lies. We feel this when Dorothy writes: "The fire flutters, and the watch ticks. I hear nothing save the breathing of my Beloved as he now and then pushes his book forward, and turns over a leaf..."

There is another entry in the Grasmere journal, which is valuable for the light it throws on Wordsworth:

We then went to John's Grove, sate a while at first; afterwards William lay, and I lay, in the trench under the fence—he with his eyes shut, and listening to the waterfalls and the birds. There was no one waterfall above another— it was a sound of waters in the air—the voice of the air. William heard me breathing, and rustling now and then, but we both lay still, and unseen by one another. He thought that it would be as sweet thus to lie so in the grave, to hear the *peaceful* sounds of the earth, and just to know that our dear friends were near.

This gives us a most rare glimpse of the real Wordsworth, not of the austere somewhat opinionated poet that the world knew, nor the joyless mutterer that the Westmorland peasantry criticised with amusing frankness, but of William Wordsworth known only to his nearest and dearest, a "Creature of a fiery heart" and of a capacity for emotion which enthralled Dorothy and which fascinated and warmed Coleridge.

IV
THE LUCY POEMS

THE LUCY POEMS

"...God be thanked, I want not society by a moonlight
lake."
DOROTHY WORDSWORTH

I have never cared greatly whether the Lucy poems
were written to Marie Anne Vallon or to Mary Hutchinson, or to some unknown maid of the Westmorland
hills. The poems themselves I have always valued so
much, because of their beauty, that the identification
of the woman around whose personality they were
written (a matter in no wise affecting their value as
poetry) seemed comparatively an uninteresting matter;
wherefore it was to me a shock to discover suddenly
that many readings of the poems, and of the Wordsworth letters and of Dorothy's journals, had left me
with the conviction, not so much that the Lucy of the
poems is Dorothy Wordsworth (for that is a misleading
way of putting the matter) but that the poems were
the fruit of the love between William and Dorothy
Wordsworth, even as the oldest tradition (a tradition
recently challenged) would have us believe.

It is not always possible (nor is it always desirable)
to prove by rule of thumb the truth of a conviction
that comes intuitively. Nevertheless, in the present
case, I find it easy to produce an amount of supporting
suggestion from the writings of Dorothy and William
Wordsworth, which, had the reasoning process come
first with me, would have led me to have a reasoned
conviction no less than an intuitive one.

M   4

This brief essay is written in the belief that, however profitless controversy as such over the subject of the Lucy poems may be, it may not be entirely profitless to use this suggestion as a commentary on the poems themselves.

The opening poem gives expression to the quite unreasonable mood of anxiety which absence from a loved one may cause. This mood merges into a kind of trance. The unreasoning and unreasonable mood is conveyed first of all through the contrast between the lover's anxiety and the apparent well-being of the loved one, who, we are told

> ...was strong and gay
> And like a rose in June,

Secondly it is conveyed by the nature of the observation, which has the sharpness shown only by the observation of a man or woman in great emotion. And thirdly it is conveyed by the symbolic tinge which this observation has. There could hardly be a more fitting choice of a symbol through which the emotion is conveyed, than the moon. And through the description of the moon sinking and sinking and sinking, until it finally disappeared behind Lucy's cottage, and of the breaking up of the trance of the lover (whose eyes have been gazing at the moon) at its disappearance, conjoined with the sudden flaring up of alarm and the broken exclamation,

> If Lucy should be dead!

Wordsworth achieves a perfect interpretation of a mood.

Analysis of the poem is tempting, as analysis of the means whereby beauty is achieved is always tempting. It is more to our present purpose, however, that such analysis shows the poem to be occasioned by exactly such a poetic stimulus as the daily life and the daily intercourse of William and Dorothy Wordsworth might produce. Their happiness when they were at Racedown and at Alfoxden had an extraordinary keenness. Of this keenness of feeling there are hints in Wordsworth's talk, as well as in his poetry. One can imagine him, on almost any moonlight night, riding towards home with vague emotions of this kind floating through his mind, and only waiting to receive poetic form. Of such emotions, apart from this poem, Wordsworth has left no actual record. As so often happens, it is in Dorothy's prose that we find illumination of his mood. For she, on quite a different occasion, has described a mood of her own that is in essence like this one. During the absence of William in June 1800, she writes: "No William! I slackened my pace as I came near home, fearing to hear that he was not come. I listened till after one o'clock to every barking dog...." We can see her, approaching the empty cottage, her steps dragging in reluctance and fear. The following day she writes:

I did not leave home, in the expectation of Wm. and John, and sitting at work till after 11 o'clock I heard a foot go to the front of the house, turn round, and open the gate. It was William! After our first joy was over, we got some tea. We did not go to bed till 4 o'clock in the morning, so he had an opportunity of seeing our improvements. The birds were singing; and all looked fresh, though not gay. There was a greyness on earth and sky.

In the poems "She dwelt among th' untrodden ways" and "Three Years she grew in sun and shower" different aspects of Dorothy's girlhood are described. Of Dorothy as she was in her maturity—shy, wild, full of intensity, fire and self-conflict—it is De Quincey who has given the unforgettable description:

"Her face was of Egyptian brown"; rarely, in a woman of English birth, had I seen a more determinate gipsy tan. Her eyes were not soft,...nor were they fierce or bold; but they were wild and startling, and hurried in their motion. Her manner was warm and even ardent; her sensibility seemed constitutionally deep; and some subtle fire of impassioned intellect apparently burned within her,...

This description tells all that can be told in prose. Wordsworth, working after the fashion of poetry, uses fewer words, but tells all. He never wrote anything purer in its outline, anything more individual yet more universal than the lines:

> She shall be sportive as the Fawn
> That wild with glee across the lawn
> Or up the mountain springs;
> And hers shall be the breathing balm,
> And hers the silence and the calm
> Of mute insensate things.
>
> The floating Clouds their state shall lend
> To her; for her the willow bend;
> Nor shall she fail to see
> Even in the motions of the Storm
> Grace that shall mould the Maiden's form
> By silent sympathy.

> The Stars of midnight shall be dear
> To her; and she shall lean her ear
> In many a secret place
> Where Rivulets dance their wayward round,
> And beauty born of murmuring sound
> Shall pass into her face.

This has the concentration of poetry. The truth of every line of it is proved in the prose of the woman who on June 1st, 1800 entered into her journal the words:

> I lay upon the steep of Loughrigg, my heart dissolved in what I saw: when I was not startled, but called from my reverie by a noise as of a child paddling without shoes. I looked up, and saw a lamb close to me. It approached nearer and nearer, as if to examine me, and stood a long time. I did not move. At last, it ran past me, and went bleating along the pathway, seeming to be seeking its mother. I saw a hare on the high road....

The poem "I travell'd among unknown Men" is an expression of tenderness coloured by nostalgia such as it was natural for Wordsworth to feel in 1799. As the presence of Dorothy makes home for him in a cold and alien land, Lucy becomes identified with England and with all that speaks of home. In this poem Wordsworth catches once more within the fine web of his poetry another of the unreasoning moods of tenderness. England is more dear to him, says the lover, in a perfectly understandable hyperbole of love, because it is upon England that Lucy's eyes have last looked.

The suggestion of death that runs throughout the poems, and comes to a climax in this poem and in the poem "A SLUMBER did my spirit seal," has its basis in the poet's brooding over death, a brooding shown in

many of the poems. As likely as not it has its immediate origin in the anxiety of the mood depicted in
the poem describing the moonlight ride of the lover,
for it is possible that the poet's imagination, trying
to give form to the vague phantoms of his feeling,
made of it a sequel to that anxiety. Wordsworth was
given to providing some such shadowy suggestion of
plot, to help him to embody his poetical impressions.
He did this with very doubtful success and with a
slightly coarsening effect, in treating the impression
which he embodied in *The Thorn*. He writes speci-
fically of the licence he allows himself in this way*, of
altering actuality so as to enable the essential impression to be embodied more substantially.

Granted that Wordsworth allowed himself this
poetic or imaginative licence, the emotion expressed
in this "most sublime epitaph," as Coleridge called it,
is of a type which we know him to have been capable
of feeling. It is just this brooding over death, and over
the oneness of the dead with Nature, and the essential
oneness of the living and the dead, that we get in those
amazing words of his on the sweetness and the communion of death, uttered to his sister as they lay
beside each other on the grass on the last Thursday
of April 1802. We get something of the same serenity
in Dorothy's description of the graveyard near Loch
Katrine:

...it was in a sloping green field among woods, and
within sound of the beating of the water against the shore,

---

* See *The Prelude*, edited by E. de Selincourt, Book VIII,
ll. 510–558.

if there were but a gentle breeze to stir it: I thought if
I lived in that house, and my ancestors and kindred were
buried there, I should sit many an hour under the walls of
this plot of earth, where all the household would be
gathered together.

It is worth recalling that Coleridge, whose intuitions
with regard to Wordsworth were seldom wrong, had
a feeling that this poem, in part mystical (for it is a description of something felt in such a moment of trance
as is described in *The Prelude*, "when the fleshly ear"
sleeps "undisturb'd"), in part emotional, in part
imaginative, was in some way connected with Dorothy.
And the words

> She seemed a thing that could not feel
> The touch of earthly years.

once more capture for us Dorothy's personality.

We know that Wordsworth used the name Lucy in
poems written about his sister. In a letter to Coleridge
in April 1802, he quotes some verses he has just
written, adding, "The incident of this poem took
place about seven years ago between Dorothy and
me." The opening verses of this poem cannot fail to
recall the first of the Lucy sheaf of poems:

> Among all lovely things my Love had been,
> Had noted well the stars, all flowers that grew
> About her home, but she had never seen
> A glow-worm, never once, and this I knew.

> While I was riding on a stormy night,
> Not far from her abode, I chanced to spy
> A single glow-worm once; and at the sight
> Down from my horse I leapt, great joy had I.

I laid the glow-worm gently on a leaf,
And bore it with me through the stormy night
In my left hand, without dismay or grief,
Shining albeit with a fainter light.

When to the dwelling of my Love I came,
I went into the orchard quietly,
And left the glow-worm, blessing it by name,
Laid safely by itself, beneath a tree *.

In the 1807 Poems, this piece, which precedes
"I travell'd among unknown Men," concludes thus:

The whole next day, I hoped, and hoped with fear;
At night the Glow-worm shone beneath the Tree:
I led my Lucy to the spot, "Look here!"
Oh! joy it was for her, and joy for me!

In tenderness, this poem which we know was written about Dorothy, is very like the Lucy poems. It is like them, too, in its lover-like wording.

We come then to the conclusion that these poems are all based on moods, emotions and states of feeling which were part of the poet's life with his sister, and which could not have been part of his life with any other woman. He whose one love sonnet, as he tells us quaintly enough, is a literary exercise, written merely to show that he too could write love poetry, gave us his real love poetry in the Lucy poems. In these poems he expresses the most romantic relationship and the deepest devotion of his life.

Wordsworth was a solitary in his love poetry. For that reason he is all the more precious, because we get

* William Knight, *Letters of the Wordsworth Family*, vol. III, p. 455.

from him what we get from no other poet. The Lucy poems owe some of their exquisiteness to their utter withdrawal from the poetry of mating. And they have a lovely quietness, rare in love poetry. Opening on a note of trance-like ecstasy, they close on a note of trance-like peace.

It is impossible not to associate with these poems the verses called *Louisa*, and that defence of the "Child of Nature" which Wordsworth associated with them in his mind. Once more it is Dorothy's prose that explains the mood in which Wordsworth writes in the verses to the "Child of Nature." Her spirited reply to her Aunt Crackanthorpe's criticism on her wanderings about the country gives us the clue. In *Louisa* we get another description of the personality described in the Lucy poems. Mr Hutchinson has indeed suggested that if any attempt be made at identification, "Louisa" should be identified with Joanna Hutchinson, firstly because "In choosing pseudonyms, the Poet always follows the principle of metrical or syllabic equi-valence,"* and secondly because the description of Louisa as being "ruddy, fleet and strong" would be more applicable to Joanna Hutchinson than to Dorothy. These statements can be easily disproved. The first of them is disproved by the verses on the glow-worm—in which we know that both Emma and Lucy are pseudonyms for Dorothy. The second is dis-proved by one of the unpublished letters of Dorothy

* *Poems in Two Volumes* by William Wordsworth, edited by T. Hutchinson, vol. i, p. 166.

herself, in which she writes compassionately of Joanna
Hutchinson's constant ill health.

Joanna Hutchinson is still with us: she was to have left
yesterday...but poor Creature! she was far too ill to go.
She has never been in strong health since she came to Grasmere or indeed, perhaps all her life not in strong health but
she has had continual headaches, with tooth-ache, and
many symptoms of nervous diseases since she came to
Grasmere and on Friday evening she had an hysteric and
a fainting fit attended with many dreadful sensations....

The description given in the *Louisa* verses has extraordinary tenderness and charm:

> And she hath smiles to earth unknown;
> Smiles, that with motion of their own
> Do spread, and sink, and rise;
> That come and go with endless play,
> And ever, as they pass away,
> Are hidden in her eyes.

This is perhaps the most intensely poetic of all the
descriptions.

The fragment defending the "Child of Nature"
against criticism has tenderness too, but it is the irony
of its ending that makes it haunting:

> Thy thoughts and feelings shall not die,
> Nor leave thee, when grey hairs are nigh,
> A melancholy slave;
> But an old age, alive and bright,
> And lovely as a Lapland night,
> Shall lead thee to thy grave.

V
IN THE WORKSHOP

IN THE WORKSHOP

"...the will never governs *his* labours."

DOROTHY WORDSWORTH

Peacock in *The Four Ages of Poetry* calls the poets of the Romantic Revival by the engaging name of "the patriarchs of the age of brass." He supposes the patriarchs of the age of brass to have communed with themselves somewhat in this wise:

Society is artificial, therefore we will live out of society. The mountains are natural, therefore we will live in the mountains. There we shall be shining models of purity and virtue, passing the whole day in the innocent and amiable occupation of going up and down hill, receiving poetical impressions and communicating them in immortal verse to admiring generations.

The caricature comes inevitably into our minds when we begin to study the poetic life of Wordsworth. Being good caricature, it is somewhat like the reality. But being caricature, it is a distortion of the reality. It does no harm, as fortunately in this case we have the reality to set beside it. Wordsworth himself gave a glimpse of the reality in the early *Prelude*, the first book of which is a matchless exposition of the "growing pains" of the poet. Dorothy Wordsworth shows us even more of the reality. She takes us right into her brother's workshop, with a freedom never permitted to the poet's contemporaries.

And extraordinarily interesting is this workshop of the poet. There are so few of the poets into whose workshops we are permitted to enter, that we may be pardoned if we linger awhile in that of Wordsworth.

The first thing we realise from this lingering is the strenuousness of the poet's calling. Wordsworth was never at rest. One of his maids, making what Professor de Selincourt calls a "pretty epigram," once told a visitor that her master's study was in the fields. The epigram contains much truth. Wherever Wordsworth was—was his workshop, and he passed most of his time out of doors. The intense driving pressure of his thought, sounding its tyrannous rhythms in his brain, brings back to the mind the words

Which way I flie is Hell; my self am Hell;

only it was not "Hell" that Wordsworth carried with him, but the need to translate into words the ecstasy, and the sense of the exquisite harmony of the universe with which his mind was flooded. Coleridge realised the intensity of the life with which his friend's hours of solitude were filled. He wrote to Poole in 1799*: "...dear Wordsworth appears to me to have hurtfully segregated and isolated his being. Doubtless his delights are more deep and sublime; but he has likewise more hours that prey upon the flesh and blood!" Wordsworth himself was perhaps conscious of this wearing, for Coleridge, when proposing in a letter to Humphry Davy in 1801 that Wordsworth and he should start the study of chemistry, wrote†: "...he

* *Letters of Samuel Taylor Coleridge*, edited by E. H. Coleridge, I, p. 297.
† *Letters of Samuel Taylor Coleridge*, edited by E. H. Coleridge, I, p. 346.

feels it more necessary for him to have some intellectual pursuit less closely connected with deep passion than poetry,..."

Dorothy makes us realise Wordsworth's experiences at this time. She makes us realise Wordsworth's joy. She makes us realise also how wearing to the poet was all this pressure of feeling, this ecstasy "too intense to be sustained." She reveals to us Wordsworth the poet, busy at his task morning, noon and night. She writes of Wordsworth on a March morning in 1802:

William... got up at nine o'clock, but before he rose he had finished *The Beggar Boy*, and while we were at breakfast... he wrote the poem *To a Butterfly*! He ate not a morsel, but sate with his shirt neck unbuttoned, and his waistcoat open while he did it. The thought first came upon him as we were talking about the pleasure we both always feel at the sight of a butterfly. I told him that I used to chase them a little, but that I was afraid of brushing the dust off their wings, and did not catch them. He told me how they used to kill all the white ones when he went to school, because they were Frenchmen.... I wrote it down and the other poems, and I read them all over to him.... William began to try to alter *The Butterfly*, and tired himself....

Again she writes in the same month:

When we came in sight of our own dear Grasmere, the vale looked fair and quiet in the moonshine, the Church was there and all the cottages. There were huge slow-travelling clouds in the sky, that threw large masses of shade upon some of the mountains. We walked backwards and forwards, between home and Olliff's, till I was tired. William kindled and began to write the poem. We carried cloaks into the orchard, and sate a while there. I left him, and he nearly finished the poem.

Some days later she writes:

I left Wm. and while he was absent I wrote out poems. I grew alarmed, and went out to seek him. I met him at Mr Olliff's. He has been trying, without success, to alter a passage—his *Silver How* poem. He had written a conclusion just before he went out. While I was getting into bed, he wrote *The Rainbow*.

A brief entry on May 14th shows that he is still troubled over the wording of *The Rainbow*: "Went to bed at half-past eleven. William very nervous. After he was in bed, haunted with altering *The Rainbow*."

Of the struggle of Wordsworth in writing *The Leech Gatherer* in May 1802 she has a great deal to say. "William had slept uncommonly well, so, feeling himself strong, he fell to work at *The Leech Gatherer*; he wrote hard at it till dinner time, then he gave over, tired to death—he had finished the poem."

Her entry of the following day shows the strength of the reaction suffered by the poet and the sister who lived in his work. "We sowed the scarlet beans in the orchard. I read *Henry V* there. William lay on his back on the seat." She adds that she wept. The note clearly shows the exhaustion of both. But *The Leech Gatherer* had not yet taken its full toll from the life of the poet. We read the entry for the morning following: "Sunday morning, 9th May.—William worked at *The Leech Gatherer* almost incessantly from morning till tea-time....I was oppressed and sick at heart, for he wearied himself to death."

The wearing of this work is shown in Wordsworth's sleeplessness. Again and again we read of Dorothy's anxiety about this. On March 12th, 1802, she writes: "In the evening after tea William wrote *Alice Fell*. He went to bed tired, with a wakeful mind and a weary body...." On April 30th, 1802, the entry is as follows. "We went to bed at 20 minutes past 11, with prayers that William might sleep well." On May 4th, Dorothy tries the old device of the lullaby. "I repeated verses to William while he was in bed; he was soothed, and I left him. 'This is the spot' over and over again."

We have just one picture of the poet at rest; it may be well to put it alongside of the record of poetic pains. It was drawn by Wordsworth himself:

> I am not One who much or oft delight
> To season my fireside with personal talk,
> About Friends, who live within an easy walk,
> Or Neighbours, daily, weekly, in my sight:
> And, for my chance-acquaintance, Ladies bright,
> Sons, Mothers, Maidens withering on the stalk,
> These all wear out of me, like Forms, with chalk
> Painted on rich men's floors, for one feast-night.
> Better than such discourse doth silence long,
> Long, barren silence, square with my desire;
> To sit without emotion, hope, or aim,
> By my half-kitchen my half-parlour fire,
> And listen to the flapping of the flame,
> Or kettle, whispering it's faint·undersong.

It is well to linger at times in the poet's workshop, not merely because of the human interest of watching a poet at work, nor even because of the realisation such

M   5

watching gives us, that Wordsworth, like every other poet, was pouring out his life in his poetry, but because as we linger we stumble upon the truth that had baffled Plato, that Shakespeare accepted with passionless quiet, that Shelley hailed as the divine distinction of poetry. This is the dependence of poetry on inspiration. "My master calls me, I must not say no," the last enigmatical word of Kent in *King Lear*, is the word of all poets. Wordsworth served a master who would brook no tarrying, who like Jehu drove furiously in his chariot, and whose words were symbols flung upon the air as he passed, and to be transcribed ere they had faded into the winds. Those who wait upon inspiration know well that the terms of their service brook no rest and no delay.

In so far as Wordsworth's poetry was an expression of the message entrusted to him to interpret, the nature of the inspiration is obvious. We see, through the poems, the poet who is shaken by his message as a reed is shaken by the wind. We see it too in those of his poems that give shape to momentary impressions. It is the exaltation caused by these impressions that is the substance of the poems. These things were all "gleams like the flashing of a shield." The poet managed to capture the gleams, which he caught when the moment of vision was on him.

What Wordsworth was like in the moments of vision Hazlitt has told us. There are two moments in observation. The first is the moment when the primrose by the river's brim is but a primrose. This is the only moment which the average man experiences. It is the moment when we behold with the fleshly eye alone. The second moment is the moment when we behold with the eye of vision. Hazlitt was once with Wordsworth when he beheld like this, and he never forgot it.

Wordsworth, looking out of the low, latticed window, said, "How beautifully the sun sets on that yellow bank!" I thought within myself "With what eyes these poets see nature!" and ever after when I saw the sunset stream upon the objects facing it, conceived I had made a discovery, or thanked Mr Wordsworth for having made one for me!*

The Solitary Reaper is one of the most beautiful of the poems which capture a moment of vision. At one moment the poet hears a girl singing. At the next the song is not one of time but of eternity. The "vale profound" is overflowing with the burden of all human experience.

The poem partakes of the infinity of poetry. It puts "a girdle round about the earth." The magic of the reaper's song like the wizard's wand places before the poet all the experience of past and present. The caverns of the grave are opened; and the dim sorrows of the past are revealed; the lonely places of the earth are brought near. Being Wordsworth, the poet brings us back after this long journey to the common light of day. And we are half-resentful at having to endure this common light.

* *My First Acquaintance with Poets.*

5-2

In the poetry that treats of the lives of men and women, the same transfiguration is found. There comes for the poet the moment when the man or woman is no longer a figure in time, but a symbol in eternity. This happens in *The Leech Gatherer*. A kind of apotheosis takes place. The old man gathering leeches is no longer merely one of the poor "old Men who have surviv'd their joy"; but a wandering figure, symbolic of patience and fortitude, and of all

> the spurnes
> That patient merit of th' unworthy takes,

The poet describes the moment of this transformation.

> While he was talking thus, the lonely place,
> The Old Man's shape, and speech, all troubled me:
> In my mind's eye I seem'd to see him pace
> About the weary moors continually,
> Wandering about alone and silently.

It is of the nature of inspiration that it is fleeting. Otherwise the poet and the seer could not live. Poetry would indeed be the blade consuming the scabbard that contained it. While it would be quite false to say that Wordsworth's vision ever quite deserted him (the Scott sonnet of 1831 is sufficient to show how Wordsworth's moments of vision came upon him in later years), it is true to say that the years during which he was most subjected to the poet's ecstasy were the marvellous ten years between 1797 and 1807. We cannot be too thankful that he waited so faithfully upon its visitations while it endured.

Its passing we can note in the successive versions of *The Prelude*, but perhaps more clearly in two of the lyrical poems. The first of these is the poem on *The Nightingale*, one of the most beautiful of Wordsworth's shorter poems. Here the poet seems to be making a definite choice, setting the quiet note of the stock-dove before the tumultuous melody of the nightingale. The other is the *Immortality Ode*, which is the swan song of Wordsworth's poetry. The burden of the *Immortality Ode* is the direct contrary of that expressed in the little poem of 1802, which inspired the ode. In 1802 Wordsworth writes:

> My heart leaps up when I behold
> A Rainbow in the sky:
> So was it when my life began;
> So is it now I am a Man;
> So be it when I shall grow old,
> Or let me die!

In the *Immortality Ode*, Wordsworth is conscious that this ecstatic keenness of feeling has gone:

> Whither is fled the visionary gleam?
> Where is it now, the glory and the dream?

But he has passed far away from the rapturous invocation to the night and the shadows in the earlier poem, should ecstasy fail:

> So be it when I shall grow old,
> Or let me die!

He tries to justify the passing of ecstasy, to show that if something has been lost, something in humanity has been gained:

The Clouds that gather round the setting sun
Do take a sober colouring from an eye
That hath kept watch o'er man's mortality;
Another race hath been, and other palms are won.
Thanks to the human heart by which we live,
Thanks to its tenderness, its joys, and fears,
To me the meanest flower that blows can give
Thoughts that do often lie too deep for tears.

Coleridge knew better. He knew in 1801, when he wrote to Godwin*, "The Poet is dead in me; my imagination...lies like a cold snuff on the circular rim of a brass candlestick," that something had gone which would return no more, and in 1802 he gathered together all his powers, all his extraordinary gift for the expression of emotion, in the lament for the passing of the "shaping spirit of Imagination."

Many reasons have been suggested for the change in Wordsworth—the sneers of the critics—the growth of worldliness. It is unlikely that these had much effect. Wordsworth had too much iron in him to be turned from his purpose by any man's sneer, and he was never worldly, although, like any man who takes unto himself a wife and begets children, he had given hostages to the world, and it may be that these links with the world helped to turn the prophet into a man. But this was not until the prophet had done a prophet's work. and the poet a poet's. It is more likely that the yoking of Wordsworth to the interests of the world followed the passing of vision, than that the passing of vision was caused by the worldliness.

* *Coleridge's Biographia Epistolaris*, I, p. 229

To blame Wordsworth for the passing of inspiration is ungrateful, as ungrateful as to blame the fire which gave warmth for a whole evening because on the following morning only its ashes are to be seen. The fire was justified by its blaze. And Wordsworth, seer and poet, is justified by the brilliance of the truth he discovered and by the brilliance of his exposition of what was truth for him in the days when he suffered himself to be broken for the purposes of the universe, when he listened, wild-eyed and haunted, to the messengers that called to him from among the mountains and tried to teach him the things that cannot be uttered.

VI
VULGAR ERRORS

VULGAR ERRORS

No one who has tried for any number of years to interpret the poetry of Wordsworth can have failed to notice that many readers come to Wordsworth's poetry bored in advance. There is only one compensation for this. The reader who has shared in the popular misconception of Wordsworth's personality and poetry experiences a startling joy in discovering suddenly that Wordsworth is a poet whose poetry has an incomparable freshness, and whose thought is bold and original.

The estimate of a poet's personality should of course have nothing to do with the reader's attitude towards his poetry, but too often unfortunately it has a great deal to do towards shaping this attitude. There are some errors, with regard to Wordsworth's personality, so widespread that they may almost be called vulgar errors, which have ranged themselves between the poet and his fit readers as those giants whom Mr Greatheart slew ranged themselves between Christiana and the promised land. Many damn Wordsworth in advance because they have lent their ears to a curious mixture of personal and poetic gossip, which, fortunately, study of the poet's life and work quickly dispels.

The first of these personal charges is that Wordsworth was egoistical beyond the measure of egoism which it is permissible and respectable for man to show. That Wordsworth had his share of egoism must be admitted, but a study of the poet's letters and of the letters of those who lived with him should at once dispel the charge of immoderate egoism. His early letters to Matthews show the extent to which he could enter into the anxieties of his friends. Throughout his life he had in friendship a delicate honour, and gave to the affairs of his friends a rare sympathy and consideration. Matthews, Terrot, Raisley Calvert, Charles and Mary Lamb were all at one time or another the objects of his solicitude. Coleridge's griefs and anxieties, and troubles of mind and body, were for many years to him as his own. His capacity for friendship is proved by the way in which his friends sought him out in their sorrows. It was to him that Basil Montagu, in great grief at the loss of his wife, turned for consolation. Dorothy writes of Montagu in 1806:

...yesterday we received a letter from him to tell us that we must not be surprized if we saw him any day, for that his wife was very ill, & that if she *should* fall a victim he feared he should lose his senses if he did not see William—therefore if he should not come down hither he begged William to go to him*.

It would not have been possible for Montagu to feel like this, if Wordsworth had not the gift of sympathy. In other letters it is of his unselfishness, his patient continuance in labour under difficult conditions that Dorothy writes. She writes to Lady Beaumont: "I cannot but admire the fortitude, and wonder at the success, with which he has laboured, in that one room,

* From an unpublished letter in the British Museum.

common to all the family, to all visitors, and where the
children frequently play beside him...." All who
were near him loved him, as they could not have loved
a man whose thoughts centred in himself. There is a
world of affection in the short phrase "such a father,"
which Dora Wordsworth uses, writing to Mrs Lawrence
in 1832.

It is Wordsworth's absorption in his writing, his
taking for granted that every detail in connection with
it is interesting, that has exposed him chiefly to this
charge, not the record of any selfish action of which he
was guilty to any of his friends or to any member of
his family, if a certain kind of selfishness be excepted
which is begotten of the very excess of love. The
absorption of the poet in his work should not have been
so misleading, for Wordsworth makes it quite clear
that his attitude is impersonal. He is absorbed in the
work not because it is his—but because he looks upon
it as something enduring and divine which it was given
to him to accomplish. He tried to make this clear from
first to last. He writes in 1800: "Having thus adverted
to a few of the reasons why I have written in verse,
and why I have chosen subjects from common life,
and endeavoured to bring my language near to the real
language of men, if I have been too minute in pleading
my own cause, I have at the same time been treating
a subject of general interest;..." He writes in 1815:

...if he* were not persuaded that the Contents of these
Volumes, and the Work to which they are subsidiary,

* Wordsworth.

evinced something of the "Vision and the Faculty divine";
and that, both in words and things, they will operate in
their degree, to extend the domain of sensibility for the
delight, the honor, and the benefit of human nature,
notwithstanding the many happy hours which he has
employed in their composition, and the manifold comforts
and enjoyments they have procured to him, he would not,
if a wish could do it, save them from immediate destruc-
tion;—from becoming at this moment, to the world, as a
thing that had never been.

Such egoism as can be brought home to Wordsworth
is mainly the egoism of the poet, based upon faith, and
capable at any moment of complete abnegation, and
at its strongest, leading to nothing more than that
frankness which in an artificial state of society pro-
duces the effect of whimsy.

The second of these personal charges is that Wordsworth was quite humorless. The letters, giving many
brief glimpses into the early days of housekeeping with
Dorothy, show that this charge is not true. Wordsworth writes to Coleridge from Grasmere, "As to the
supper-cake which I promised, it died of a very
common malady, bad advice. The oven must be hot,
perfectly hot, said Molly the experienced, so into a
piping red-hot oven it went, and came out (but I hate
antithesis, in colours especially) black as a genuine
child of the coal-hole. In plain English, it is not a
sendable article." Dorothy's descriptions of his re-
lations with his children also go far to refute the
charge. The springs of laughter are not dried up in the
man who called his son John's tongue "the Dragon of
Wantley" in his den. Occasionally his prose shows

a quiet humour, as in his mischievous description of men of mature age "thinking it proper that their understandings should enjoy a holiday, while they are unbending their minds with verse,..." The description of the tea-party in *Peter Bell* is a masterpiece of sardonic humour:

> Is it a party in a parlour?
> Cramm'd just as they on earth were cramm'd—
> Some sipping punch, some sipping tea,
> But, as you by their faces see,
> All silent and all damn'd!

But even this should not be needed, nor the grim-grotesque humour of other parts of *Peter Bell*, nor the mischief of some of the occasional verses, nor the parody of *Queen and Huntress* which Dorothy enclosed in a letter to Mrs Clarkson; for in one very beautiful and fanciful poem on the Daisy, Wordsworth has given expression to a humour compounded of many simples, of which perhaps the chief is tenderness. It is impossible to read this poem without unbending to the quietly freakish humour. Wordsworth is for once lavish in eccentric and tender embellishment. His "web of similies" for the flower of "homely face" is a masterpiece of teasing affection:

> A Nun demure of lowly port,
> Or sprightly Maiden of Love's Court,
> In thy simplicity the sport
>   Of all temptations;
> A Queen in crown of rubies drest,
> A Starveling in a scanty vest,
> Are all, as seem to suit thee best,
>   Thy appellations.

A little Cyclops, with one eye
Staring to threaten and defy,
That thought comes next—and instantly
    The freak is over,
The shape will vanish, and behold!
A silver Shield with boss of gold,
That spreads itself, some Faery bold
    In fight to cover.

The third charge made against Wordsworth is that he was dull. But this charge is only made by those who never drew near to the poet. Wordsworth possessed the intense magnetism which accompanies the capacity for powerful feeling. Those who drew near to him were bound to him for ever by this magnetism, a magnetism so strong that not even the counter-magnetism of Coleridge could prevail against it: when Coleridge and Wordsworth drew apart, it is significant that it was Wordsworth who retained the allegiance not only of Dorothy, but of Sara Hutchinson.

The fourth charge is that Wordsworth was soft in grain. It is partly because of the nickname bestowed by Fitzgerald that this charge is so often made. A phrase like "Daddy Wordsworth" is a regular old man of the sea. Even the many contemporary descriptions of Wordsworth's appearance, however, correct the impression given by it. Hazlitt's description of Wordsworth as he was in 1798, "gaunt and Don Quixote-like," gives the impression of a man anything but soft.

There was a severe, worn pressure of thought about his temples, a fire in his eye (as if he saw something in objects more than the outward appearance), an intense, high, narrow forehead, a Roman nose, cheeks furrowed by strong purpose and feeling, and a convulsive inclination to laughter about the mouth, a good deal at variance with the solemn, stately expression of the rest of his face*.

Coleridge, in a letter to Sir George Beaumont, implies that Wordsworth's face was noticeably hard. Carlyle's description makes use of the same word. "His face bore marks of much, not always peaceful, meditation; the look of it not bland or benevolent so much as close impregnable and hard:..." † Even the brief but pungent description of the Westmorland peasant conveys some impression of hardness: "He was a ugly-faäced man, and a meän liver." ‡

These give their impressions in the way of prose. It may not be altogether fanciful to think that we get the best of all descriptions of Wordsworth from his own lines on Peter Bell:

> There was a hardness in his cheek,
> There was a hardness in his eye,
> As if the man had fix'd his face,
> In many a solitary place,
> Against the wind and open sky!

That Wordsworth in his life, and in the choices he made, showed the hardness of character which the expression of his face would seem to indicate cannot be doubted. Carlyle, whose respect was only rendered to personalities that had a touch of iron in them, noted

* *My First Acquaintance with Poets.*

† *Reminiscences by Thomas Carlyle*, edited by J. A. Froude, II, *Appendix*, p. 333.

‡ H. D. Rawnsley, *Reminiscences of Wordsworth amongst the Peasantry of Westmoreland.*

M   6

the touch of hardness when he met the poet. Wordsworth was a man who took his risks. Because of this hardness of character he successfully resisted the attempts of his uncles to make him choose a profession. And it was his hardness of fibre that helped him through the succeeding years of poverty. In his youth he was unworldly to the point of quixotry. Moreover, he believed that poetry could only be understood by those who were not of this world. He himself obeyed almost literally the command to "take no thought for the morrow." He was poor and his living was scanty. In 1795 he wrote: "I have lately been living upon air, and the essence of carrots, cabbages, turnips, and other esculent vegetables,—not excluding parsley, the produce of my garden." Cottle, who visited Wordsworth in 1798, gives an impression of the poet's life which makes us realise the extreme bareness of the living. His description also makes us realise how joyously the Wordsworths battled with poverty. Coleridge too gives us a glimpse of the joy this austere life could have, when he writes in 1800:*

We drank tea the night before I left Grasmere, on the island in that lovely lake; our kettle swung over the fire, hanging from the branch of a fir-tree, and I lay and saw the woods, and mountains, and lake all trembling, and as it were idealized through the subtle smoke, which rose up from the clear, red embers of the fir-apples which we had collected: afterwards we made a glorious bonfire on the margin, by some elder bushes, whose twigs heaved and sobbed in the uprushing column of smoke, and the image of the bonfire, and of us that danced round it, ruddy, laughing faces in the twilight;...

    * *Coleridge's Biographia Epistolaris*, i, pp. 200–1.

We gather from a letter written by Dorothy to Mrs Clarkson in July 1803 that these joys were not interrupted at first by Wordsworth's marriage. Even the baby is a sunburnt gipsy. Dorothy writes:

> The Child sleeps all night, & is a very good sleeper in the day,—I wish you could see him in his Basket, which is neither more nor less than a meat Basket, which cost half a crown. In this basket he has floated over Grasmere water asleep, not like Moses in his cradle of Rushes, but in a boat, mind that now, and made one of a dinner party at the Island....

The Wordsworths wore their poverty with grace. Yet though Wordsworth, during these joyous although perilous days, had "courage," in what he himself calls the Chaucerian sense of the word (that courage which in 1832 he confessed to Rowan Hamilton he had left behind him), the uncertainty took its toll from him. Wordsworth's early poetry is marked with the consciousness of the risks he took. It is the man who is insecure of fortune who sees his face at the bottom of every pond. It is the poet who is insecure of fortune whose unguided thoughts take the form shown in *The Leech Gatherer*, the broodings over "mighty Poets in their misery dead," over

> ...Chatterton, the marvellous Boy,
> The sleepless Soul that perish'd in its pride;

these lines betray the anxiety that Wordsworth, choosing deliberately insecurity of fortune and tenacious of his choice, was too stubborn to express more explicitly. His life was not soft. He chose insecurity of fortune because he believed that he had a message to deliver. In the same way he chose the hermit life,

6-2

because in that life he found himself in closest contact
with the things that were reality to him. But the hermit
life is not easy. The record kept by Dorothy of Wordsworth's poetic strivings during these days of withdrawal from the world is in itself sufficient to show
that the life of contemplation, worthily lived, is the
hardest life of all. It meant for the poet the facing of
his own soul and his relationship to the universe, and
that is a problem which few dare face, to avoid facing
which man keeps himself busy with all sorts of in-
essentials. We

> ...see all sights from pole to pole,
> And glance, and nod, and bustle by;
> And never once possess our soul
> Before we die.

Wordsworth went straight to essentials. That is why,
to the shallow man, who is conscious only of the super-
ficial trappings of existence, his life seemed easy. To
such an observer, and especially to the man who has
never wrestled with creative work, St John on Patmos
would seem to be having a perpetual holiday; for the
man who has never wrestled with the forces of creation
does not know their almost malignant strength. When
the work done in solitude appears, those who can read
it in a night are apt to forget that it is not the work of
a night, but the fruit of tireless brooding and of a
chaos of mental disquiet with which the poet has
wrestled until from it he has brought forth sweetness
and light.

VII
A COMMENTARY ON WORDSWORTH'S
THEORY OF POETIC DICTION

A COMMENTARY ON WORDSWORTH'S THEORY OF POETIC DICTION

"I am not a critic, and set little value upon the art."

WORDSWORTH

"I found that Herder agreed with Wordsworth as to poetical language."

CRABB ROBINSON

It is the strength and the weakness of Wordsworth's criticism that it centres in himself. He was too absorbed in his own work to judge fairly of the work of other men always, and he was not primarily interested in criticism. Occasionally he lets fall an interesting remark such as that Skelton was "a demon in point of genius." He writes of Milton: "However imbued the surface might be with classical literature, he was a Hebrew in soul;" it is he who utters the final judgment on the place of Pope and Dryden in poetry; his analysis of the sonnet is excellent. But in the main he has little to say of his predecessors that is remarkable or illuminating. And he could not take the measure of his contemporaries. He misunderstood Coleridge's finest poem; he undervalued Scott; he failed to give Byron his due.

His criticism of his own work, however, is most illuminating, and most of his criticism is inspired directly or indirectly by his own poetry. His analysis of some of the lines of *The Leech Gatherer*, written to illustrate the operation of the imagination, shows how he brooded over his work. The result of this brooding is also shown in the penetrating analysis of the sonnet, "With Ships the sea was sprinkled far and nigh." This analysis is really an exquisite piece of work. And when we come to the critical essays, which are the result of introspection, we come to work of great value. If read, as they were meant to be read, along with the poems they were meant to expound, these pieces, a poet's commentary on his own poetry and a poet's statement of poetic faith, have something of that freshness which Coleridge claimed for his friend's poetry. They are sometimes fumbling. They take some time in expressing the poet's full meaning. But their eagerness, their freshness makes itself felt even through the weariness of most of the critical commentaries which envelop them, rather than interpret them. Coleridge himself did not quite get at the heart of Wordsworth's meaning.

Wordsworth began with a very unassuming attempt to explain the nature of his experiments in poetry. He professed to be making the experiment which Chaucer (wisely refraining from or perhaps not caring for theoretical exposition) had made before him in *The Canterbury Tales*. He passed on to deeper and more searching work, towards analysis of the nature of poetry and all its works. It must be remembered that he was making paths in new territory, and feeling his way. There are times when he is clumsy in his way of expressing himself, and his final teaching (never retracted by him, as his letter to John Abraham Heraud in 1830 shows) is given not in one Preface, nor in another, but in all this writing taken together. The reader should remember to look consistently for the meaning, which is trying to beat its way out through words that sometimes almost obscure it, rather than to attempt to look too closely at the letter of the word itself.

This commentary is an attempt to state simply what Wordsworth has said in these pieces on the vexed question of poetic diction, and to defend his central position. Before proceeding to a statement of Wordsworth's views on poetic diction, it is necessary to pause for a moment to call to memory what his conception of poetry itself was.

Wordsworth's brooding over the nature of poetry led him to the conclusion that poetry is something which is not made captive exclusively by either of the formal divisions of literature, prose or verse. It is from this central belief that his theory of poetic diction springs.

This belief of his is misrepresented by contemporary wit in the lines describing Wordsworth as one

> Who, both by precept and example, shows
> That prose is verse, and verse is merely prose;

The misrepresentation is obvious, for Wordsworth is careful to indicate that he is not primarily concerned either with verse or with prose. These are terms representing formal distinctions, and he is careful to emphasise the formal distinctions, but gives us to understand that his chief concern is with the kind of writing (to be found both in the regular rhythms which constitute verse and in the irregular rhythms

which constitute prose) whose *differentia* it is, not that
the words are in regular rhythm or without regular
rhythm, but that they have the power of bringing the
subject of which they treat *sub specie aeternitatis*. This
is what Wordsworth means by poetry. And this kind
of writing is found either in verse or prose. Those who
can write in this way are poets, whether they prefer to
confine themselves to the regular rhythm of verse, or no.

In the sense in which Wordsworth uses the word,
Plato is a poet, and Lord Bacon (even as Shelley has
it), and Mr Synge, and the writer of the close of *The
Woodlanders*.

It is entirely natural that from this conception of
poetry Wordsworth should pass on to his most
challenged conclusion, that there neither is nor can be
any essential difference between the language of
poetry conveyed through the medium of prose and the
language of poetry conveyed through the medium of
verse. In either case the language is "a selection of the
language really spoken by men."

But, it must be remembered, this conclusion is one
that leaves ample liberty of selection. Between the
language of man and man there is as much variation
sometimes as between the language of man and that
of creatures of another planet. And "selection" is
a word that admits of a wide interpretation. It was
really not necessary for Coleridge to narrow down all
that Wordsworth implied in the word "selection," by
stating that the language of poetry demanded a
severer keeping. For it is impossible to dogmatise on

the suitability of individual words for poetry. The
suitability is entirely a matter of the moment. And
words can play strange tricks. A word that has an air
of perfect rightness in one poem will look grotesque in
another. Thus "cows" would be classed among the
neutral words in poetry. But its neutrality depends
entirely on the remainder of the poem in which it is
placed. In Mr Masefield's beautiful verse:

> All through the windless night the clipper rolled
> In a great swell with oily gradual heaves
> Which rolled her down until her time-bells tolled,
> Clang, and the weltering water moaned like beeves.
> The thundering rattle of slatting shook the sheaves,
> Startles of water made the swing ports gush,
> The sea was moaning and sighing and saying "Hush!"

the substitution of "cows" for "beeves" would have
a suggestion of incongruousness sufficient to wreck the
verse.

It is impossible to dogmatise as to which words are
right and which are not. The word "selection" gives
all the guidance that is necessary.

It was indeed part of Wordsworth's belief * that this
"selection" should include the language of simple men,
and this belief brought him much ridicule. But he has

---

* Sir Walter Scott, who shared Wordsworth's belief in
the rightness of the language of simple men when moved by
great emotion, justified his faith with uncommon power.
The words of Saunders Mucklebackit on returning to work
after lamenting the death of his son in a storm at sea have
some of the inevitability of the words in which David
lamented Absalom: "It's weel wi' you gentles, that can
sit in the house wi' hand-kerchers at your een when ye lose
a friend; but the like o' us maun to our wark again, if our
hearts were beating as hard as my hammer."

the support of literature. It is just this kind of beauty that we get in the closing scene of *King Lear*. It is this kind of beauty that we get in some of the great moments of the sagas. Of this kind of beauty there is one remarkable instance in the first volume of that modern saga, Mr Andersen Nexö's *Pelle Erobreren*. The old fisherman Ole has come out to look for his brave son Niels, who has been drowned in attempting to effect an impossible rescue on the sea. When the body is brought to him, his words are: "Han har roet godt! Blodet er traadt ud af Fingerenderne,..."* This is one of the rare precious simplicities of literature. Mr Synge's plays show some of this beauty. And their rhythm "was caught from the voices of fishers in Aran, shaken by fear or bereavement."† Mr Masefield's *Nan* has this kind of beauty. There is beauty in the broken rhythm of the Gaffer's speech. "Singing. Singing. Roaring it come. Roaring it come. Over the breast. Over the lips. Over the eyes."

It is a kind of beauty that is not dependent on time, or place, or conventions of art, for it is the beauty of the living voice. We get it as unmistakably in the words of the mediaeval English poet:

> Is that your los? By god, hit is routhe!

or in the words of the mediaeval German poet:

> Kuste er mich? Wol tusentstunt!
> tantaradei!
> Seht wie rot mir ist der munt,

---

* "He's rowed well: the blood's come out at his finger tips."   † C. E. Montague, *Dramatic Values*.

as in the

      da mi basia mille, deinde centum,

of Catullus, or the

        ἔγω δὲ μόνα κατεύδω.

of Sappho.

These examples have been chosen to show the wide application of Wordsworth's conclusion. There are many examples to be found in his own poetry, and in the poetry of Coleridge, whose simplicities are divine.

But a belief that poetry may be found in the language of simple men, and a belief in the value of the poetry that had this kind of simplicity, is only part of the poetic faith of Wordsworth, who is careful to guard against any suspicion that he wishes to confine poetry to this simplicity. These safeguards erected by Wordsworth himself are too often forgotten. Those who point with triumph to his more stately poems and say that Wordsworth writes well when he forgets his theory, have read Wordsworth's confession of faith but superficially. Wordsworth holds no brief for simplicity. A "selection" of the real language of men is not necessarily composed of simple words, although it may include simple words. Wordsworth knows that all men do not express themselves simply under emotion, that all poets even do not. If he had thought they did, he could not have loved Milton's poetry with a life-long love. A "selection" of the real language of men may be ornate and splendid. Thus Wordsworth leaves scope for the splendour of language which character-

ises some poems, and the poet in some of his moods.
The poet is a man addressing himself to men. His
utterance may be simple or it may be magnificent.
That depends on the man who is the poet. Wordsworth's own poetry shows the two extremes. At one
time it is natural for him to use the quiet phrasing of
the Lucy poems. At another time it is natural for him
to raise his voice in the stately chant of the *Immortality
Ode*. This expression is decorative. He chooses the
statelier mode even although he has before him the
lines in which Coleridge gave expression to the same
emotion:

> There was a time when earth, and sea, and skies,
> The bright green vale, and forest's dark recess,
> With all things, lay before mine eyes
>   In steady loveliness:

these have a steadier and a quieter beauty.

Sometimes in the course of one of Wordsworth's
poems we get the two kinds of beauty combined.
Wordsworth draws a distinction between poetry that
is dramatic (where the words must suit the speaker) and
poetry in which, whether it be lyrical or meditative,
the poet, a man speaking to men, utters the speech of
his heart. These kinds of poetry sometimes unite in the
one poem, and then we get the contrast between the
words of the subject of the poem (usually simple in
character) and the words of the poet himself. This
contrast between the language of the author and the
language (no less beautiful but different in kind) of one
of his characters may be illustrated from the ending

of *The Woodlanders*, an illustration which, we believe, would have pleased Wordsworth himself.

As this solitary and silent girl stood there in the moonlight, a straight slim figure, clothed in a plaitless gown, the contours of womanhood so undeveloped as to be scarcely perceptible, the marks of poverty and toil effaced by the misty hour, she touched sublimity at points, and looked almost like a being who had rejected with indifference the attribute of sex for the loftier quality of abstract humanism. She stooped down and cleared away the withered flowers that Grace and herself had laid there the previous week, and put her fresh ones in their place.

'Now, my own, own love,' she whispered, 'you are mine, and on'y mine; for she has forgot'ee at last, although for her you died! But I—whenever I get up I'll think of 'ee, and whenever I lie down I'll think of 'ee. Whenever I plant the young larches I'll think that none can plant as you planted; and whenever I split a gad, and whenever I turn the cider wring, I'll say none could do it like you. If ever I forget your name let me forget home and heaven!...But no, no, my love, I never can forget 'ee; for you was a good man, and did good things!'

Here we have the words of Mr Hardy first of all, and secondly the words of Marty South. And both speeches are poetical in character, although the one is anything but simple, and the other has all a peasant's simplicity.

Wordsworth has sometimes been blamed for his half-hearted words on Coleridge's brilliant exposition of his principles and poetry in the *Biographia Literaria*. The half-heartedness is explained when we remember that Coleridge judged him by the letter of the word. This must have been disappointing to Wordsworth, who might have hoped that if all others misunderstood him Coleridge might have penetrated through anything that was fumbling in his words to the meaning beneath.

We come to the conclusion, then, that Wordsworth's successive utterances make quite clear what he wished to say with regard to poetic diction, that his pronouncement shows the essentially meditative character of his mind, and that it was justified.

One of the most usual modes of attack on Wordsworth's theory is to confront the poet with his less successful poems, and to use these to show that the theory is wrong. This is unfair. The same criticism might be made against Coleridge, who wrote doggerel at times, but whose simplicities at other times "touched sublimity." Wordsworth himself has given the answer to these critics in the comment in his *Appendix* on the Alexander Selkirk poem. The pieces that fail are not only bad poetry. They would be equally ineffective in prose.

It may be mentioned in this connection that some of the pieces pilloried by Mr Hutchinson as showing the evil effect of Wordsworth's theory upon his practice are not as ineffective as he would seem to indicate. *Alice Fell*, *Beggars* (which Sara Coleridge noted as having "some power about it"), and *The Sailor's Mother* all succeed in suggesting the rhythm of life. They give pleasure of a kind. What is wrong with them is that they bear upon them the marks of a twice-told tale. The incidents on which they were based had already been expressed in the inevitable words of Dorothy's journal. It was a mistake to try to mould her words into regular rhythms, although a mistake natural enough for Wordsworth, who valued very highly the charm of verse.

It is peculiarly fitting that it should fall to the lot of the brother of such an artist in prose and such a poet at heart as Dorothy Wordsworth was, to remind a world divorced from poetic reality that the language of poetry is one and indivisible, whether for the moment it speaks in words tumultuous and sublime, or whether it "singeth a quiet tune," whether it measures its rhythms according to an accepted pattern, or whether the harmonies it creates are as little susceptible of formal measuring as the harmonies of the spheres.

VIII

THE SUBSTANCE OF WORDSWORTH'S POETRY

THE SUBSTANCE OF WORDSWORTH'S POETRY

> "I wish to keep my Reader in the company of flesh and blood,..."
>
> *Preface of* 1800

The substance of Wordsworth's poetry was largely conditioned by four chance circumstances. The first of these is that his childhood was a most unusual one—the second that he had passed through a revolution—the third that he had betrayed (however unintentionally) a woman—the fourth that he had suffered under the influence of a philosophy ruinous to a man of his spiritual constitution.

The childhood of the artist is always important; Wordsworth's was even more important than is usually the case. Much of his time was spent in listening to the music of the universe among the hills. He writes:

> Fair seed-time had my soul, and I grew up
> Foster'd alike by beauty and by fear;

In *The Prelude* he tells of the experiences of his boyhood. He writes thus of the song of the winds:

> Oh! when I have hung
> Above the raven's nest, by knots of grass
> And half-inch fissures in the slippery rock
> But ill sustain'd, and almost, as it seem'd,
> Suspended by the blast which blew amain,
> Shouldering the naked crag; Oh! at that time,
> While on the perilous ridge I hung alone,
> With what strange utterance did the loud dry wind
> Blow through my ears!

He describes the emotional after-effect on him of the
boyish dishonesty of robbing the snares set by one of
his companions:

> ...when the deed was done
> I heard among the solitary hills
> Low breathings coming after me, and sounds
> Of undistinguishable motion, steps
> Almost as silent as the turf they trod.

His hauntings among the hills by august and shadowy
forces are very beautifully described in the lines in
which he tells of the escapade of the boat:

> One evening (surely I was led by her)*
> I went alone into a Shepherd's Boat,
> A Skiff that to a Willow tree was tied
> Within a rocky Cave, its usual home.
> 'Twas by the shores of Patterdale, a Vale
> Wherein I was a Stranger, thither come
> A School-boy Traveller, at the Holidays.
> Forth rambled from the Village Inn alone
> No sooner had I sight of this small Skiff,
> Discover'd thus by unexpected chance,
> Than I unloos'd her tether and embark'd.
> The moon was up, the Lake was shining clear
> Among the hoary mountains; from the Shore
> I push'd, and struck the oars and struck again
> In cadence, and my little Boat mov'd on
> Even like a Man who walks with stately step
> Though bent on speed. It was an act of stealth
> And troubled pleasure; not without the voice
> Of mountain-echoes did my Boat move on,
> Leaving behind her still on either side
> Small circles glittering idly in the moon,
> Until they melted all into one track

* Nature.

Of sparkling light. A rocky Steep uprose
Above the Cavern of the Willow tree
And now, as suited one who proudly row'd
With his best skill, I fix'd a steady view
Upon the top of that same craggy ridge,
The bound of the horizon, for behind
Was nothing but the stars and the grey sky.
She was an elfin Pinnace; lustily
I dipp'd my oars into the silent Lake,
And, as I rose upon the stroke, my Boat
Went heaving through the water, like a Swan;
When from behind that craggy Steep, till then
The bound of the horizon, a huge Cliff,
As if with voluntary power instinct
Uprear'd its head. I struck, and struck again
And, growing still in stature, the huge Cliff
Rose up between me and the stars, and still,
With measur'd motion, like a living thing,
Strode after me. With trembling hands I turn'd,
And through the silent water stole my way
Back to the Cavern of the Willow tree.
There, in her mooring-place, I left my Bark,
And through the meadows homeward went, with grave
And serious thoughts; and after I had seen
That spectacle, for many days, my brain
Work'd with a dim and undetermin'd sense
Of unknown modes of being; in my thoughts
There was a darkness, call it solitude,
Or blank desertion, no familiar shapes
Of hourly objects, images of trees,
Of sea or sky, no colours of green fields;
But huge and mighty Forms that do not live
Like living men mov'd slowly through the mind
By day and were the trouble of my dreams.

The French Revolution was of importance in determining the substance of Wordsworth's poetry, because

it brought the poet face to face with reality, and forced him to divest himself of the inhumanity of a youth preoccupied with Nature. That which he had to say must henceforth be related to men, and must deal with Man. It was necessary that the foundations of his poetry should be laid among the hills, but Wordsworth had to mingle with people before he could relate his message to their needs. After this mingling, he was never a recluse in the sense of the word which implies a selfish withdrawal from the interests of men. He was always conscious of the times, and every line of poetry he wrote was written with the needs of men in his mind.

No less important than the French Revolution in assisting Wordsworth to discard his inhumanity was his enforced desertion of Marie Anne Vallon, followed by long anguish and remorse. Even in his early manhood the poet might have written:

A deep distress hath humaniz'd my Soul.

Each of these things assisted the poet's development in a positive way. The first gave him the foundations of his poetry; the second taught him to cast that poetry into the form of a message for his fellow-men; the third softened him and rendered his nature accessible. The fourth determining circumstance was the influence of Godwin upon Wordsworth, and its operation was different. It acted as an irritant, and it was in the reaction from it that Wordsworth found his true strength. There came a time when rejecting the teaching of

Godwin he described thus the tyranny of reason which
he had endured:

> Thus I fared,
> Dragging all passions, notions, shapes of faith,
> Like culprits to the bar,....

He tells of the sickness of heart which followed:

> ......I lost
> All feeling of conviction, and, in fine,
> Sick, wearied out with contrarieties,
> Yielded up moral questions in despair,

What the study of the mystics did for Coleridge,
Nature did for Wordsworth in this crisis. His final re-
jection of the teaching of Godwin made him see quite
clearly that the thing which mattered for him was the
experience of his youth, and the interpreting it to
assuage the world's sorrow. Suddenly he realised that
he had a message, and that his whole life had prepared
him for delivering this message. For many an artist
"the wayes of God to men" have been justified by
this sudden realisation. Wordsworth acknowledged the
help given by Dorothy in this realisation of his true
strength and his true task:

> She, in the midst of all, preserv'd me still
> A Poet, made me seek beneath that name
> My office upon earth, and nowhere else,

Every poet is perhaps a seer. Wordsworth is a seer
in a special sense. We do not begin to understand him
until we realise that he is a seer, believing intensely in
his vision. He writes:

> Possessions have I that are solely mine,
> Something within which yet is shared by none,

Not even the nearest to me and most dear,
Something which power and effort may impart;
I would impart it, I would spread it wide:
Immortal in the world which is to come—
Forgive me if I add another claim—
And would not wholly perish even in this,
Lie down and be forgotten in the dust,
I and the modest Partners of my days
Making a silent company in death;
Love, knowledge, all my manifold delights,
All buried with me without monument
Or profit unto any but ourselves!
It must not be, if I, divinely taught,
Be privileged to speak as I have felt
Of what in man is human or divine.

It was about 1795 that Wordsworth began to understand his own message, and to try to utter it. After a mighty struggle, he succeeded. He set it down for us with a simplicity which is a constant snare to the vulgar. He felt that the poet, unlike the minstrel of old who sang to the people, had drawn away from the people. He himself attempted anew the minstrel's function, drawing near to the people. Thus he began by singing a simple song. But his simplicity was the true golden simplicity. It was a simplicity of expression, not a simplicity of thought. Unlike some poets, who have said simple things in a difficult way, he uttered difficult things in the simplest of words.

He is successful in his utterance even in the *Lyrical Ballads* of 1798. Four volumes which he published during his lifetime give us the key to his thought—the

Lyrical Ballads of 1798, the *Lyrical Ballads* of 1800,
and the two volumes of 1807. In these volumes we
have the pure gold of Wordsworth's poetry. *The
Prelude*, written between 1795 and 1805, is his fullest
confession of faith, but it was not published in the poet's
lifetime. The fragment of *The Recluse*, not published
till 1875, is the most illuminating of all his poems.

The poet's quarry was human nature, and the poet's
principal object was "to follow the fluxes and refluxes
of the mind when agitated by the great and simple
affections of our nature."* In setting about to accomplish this object he began by the investigation of what
for him was reality. He wished to build his poetry on
a sure basis, on what he actually knew. Wordsworth
was scrupulously sincere. Gradually he succeeded in
beating out his personal message, his personal conception of life, and this must be understood before the
remainder of Wordsworth's poetry is understood, for
the remainder is built on this.

He realised that certain of his childhood's experiences
were the very gift of God to him. These experiences
taught him that the beauty of the visible universe is
one of God's best gifts to men—and that from communion with this beauty, the spirit of man can be
interpenetrated with the spirit of the Creator, and
caught into an ecstasy, while the body is in a trance.
It is this that Wordsworth tries to express in the semi-
mystical verses "A SLUMBER did my spirit seal." This
is the faith of Wordsworth the mystic, and this was his

* *Preface of* 1800.

message for his times. The man who lived wholly in the world missed this communion:

> The world is too much with us; late and soon,
> Getting and spending, we lay waste our powers:

but the complete man must listen to these voices.

In his *Lines Written A Few Miles Above Tintern Abbey* Wordsworth tries to explain the progression of his belief, tracing it from the first days when his delight in Nature was merely animal, to the days when he became conscious that something spiritual in Nature was sending its message to his spirit, and from that to the days when he felt that his own spirit was drawn into this spirit and identified with it. It is the power of Nature to communicate its message in its own way that he tries to explain in *Expostulation and Reply*, a poem which is an answer to the man who reproached him for dreaming his time away:

> The eye it cannot choose but see;
> We cannot bid the ear be still;
> Our bodies feel, where'er they be,
> Against, or with our will.
>
> Nor less I deem that there are powers
> Which of themselves our minds impress;
> That we can feed this mind of ours
> In a wise passiveness.
>
> Think you, 'mid all this mighty sum
> Of things for ever speaking,
> That nothing of itself will come,
> But we must still be seeking?
>
> —Then ask not wherefore, here, alone,
> Conversing as I may,
> I sit upon this old gray stone,
> And dream my time away.

This message, based on Wordsworth's personal communion with Nature, may seem somewhat divested
of humanity. But the poet proceeded to relate it to
humanity. The remainder of his poetry, both that
dealing with what we call the inanimate things of
Nature, and that dealing with human beings, follows
naturally from this central belief. It follows from this
belief of Wordsworth (that through communion with
Nature we can have communion with the Creator)—
that all sorts of little things, making up the visible
universe, are of importance. It was one of the crit-
icisms often levelled at Wordsworth that he dealt with
trivialities. But to the poet trivialities did not exist.
He was like Browning's Lazarus. He had the mystic's
view of life. Things which thrilled the ordinary man
left him unmoved. Things which the ordinary man
trod underfoot were to him symbols of eternity. For
him all things were

> Bound by gold chains about the feet of God.

The daisy had its message, its "function apostolical,"
as the poet put it. The words are exactly right. The
celandine and the daffodils had their work to perform.
The morning mist. and the Sun "new ris'n," as it

> Looks through the Horizontal misty Air,

are all part of a great whole. The wild things of the
earth are the poet's kin:

> Friends shall I have at dawn, blackbird and thrush
> To rouse me, and a hundred warblers more!

Nothing is too mean to share in this brotherhood.

Wordsworth is like Blake in this respect. Reading him, we think inevitably of the sweet and poignant words of the *Book of Thel*, in which Thel communes with all creation, and of the lines from *The Four Zoas*:

> Arise, you little glancing wings & sing your
> infant joy,
> Arise & drink your bliss!
> For everything that lives is holy;

When the poet deals with men and women, he carries the same spirit into his dealing. All men and women are the objects of his poetic vision. He saw the poetry in the lives of humble folk. For this the bewildered critics, concealing their bewilderment by making merry over his "drunken skylarks" and "fiery nightingales," despised him. Goody Blake and Harry Gill, Lucy Gray, the haunting dream child, Alice Fell, broken-hearted at the loss of her cloak, Simon Lee and the Leech Gatherer, the old Cumberland Beggar and other brave and pathetic old men, and a host of folk humble as those through whom Mr Hardy illustrates the tragi-comedy of life, display the action of the forces of life in Wordsworth's pages.

There are few poets whose work is so integral as Wordsworth's. Once we understand the belief that moved him, each shorter piece falls into place. This is not sufficiently realised. The critic who has not studied Wordsworth closely is frequently misleading on this point. He thinks he knows Wordsworth when he has read a few of the poems. This is not so. Wordsworth himself was never tired of emphasising the unity of his work. The poetry of his creative years cannot be read in selection. And his poems have a deceptive simplicity. Many who think they understand them have failed to press out of them their full meaning, because they have not related the parts to the whole. Wordsworth is a proud poet, and jealous of the dignity of poetry. He permits no one to make progress in his meaning "like an Indian prince or General—stretched on his Palanquin, and borne by his Slaves." He has nothing for critics "too petulant to be passive to a genuine Poet, and too feeble to grapple with him;..." It is only after we have tirelessly followed him in his soarings and in his descents into humdrum places, until we have come close to him and grappled with him, only after we have explored the whole region of his winging, that we can hope to understand this poet, or the least of his works.

IX

ON THE DEPRECIATION OF
WORDSWORTH'S POETRY

ON THE DEPRECIATION OF
WORDSWORTH'S POETRY

"They are *fresh* and have the dew upon them."

COLERIDGE

"There is something morbid, as if shrinking from human contact, in the nature worship of Wordsworth,..."

MRS VIRGINIA WOOLF

These two fragments of criticism might be taken to illustrate the "gulph of separation" that exists between the true and natural interpretation of poetry, and the artificial and false. It is well to remember this sentence from Coleridge's exposition of his friend's work, because, apart from the barriers cast in the way of arriving at a just estimate of Wordsworth's poetry by the misinterpretation of the poet's personality, the chief obstacle is just that the freshness of the poetry has been obscured.

In analysing the causes of the disfavour into which Wordsworth's poetry has fallen, we realise at once that some of the poems suffer from being hackneyed. We seem always to have known them. Not only has the familiarity dimmed their beauty, but their meaning was lost because we came to them before we had any conception of the whole of which they were a part. They were staled before they were understood.

Such objection to Wordsworth's poetry as is based upon this unfortunate staling may be at once dismissed as an unreal objection.

8-2

Another reason for dislike is that (because there is so much talk about Nature in Wordsworth's poetry) the belief has gone abroad that the poetry is lacking in humanity. This, too, is an unreal objection, and one which is of little importance, as the poetry needs only to be studied for this impression to find correction. The poet deals with his own life, and the lives among which his lot was cast. Poems like *The Happy Warrior*, *Brougham Castle*, the *Elegiac Verses*, and part of the last book of *The Prelude*, dissipate instantly this impression.

A third reason for dislike is Wordsworth's occasional verbal infelicity, which all fools think it worth their while to point out—as well as many who are anything but fools.

Other things that work against the enjoyment of Wordsworth's poetry are that he had the drawbacks of his own good points. One of the first things we look for in a great writer, and one of the things we invariably find, is the kind of earnestness to which Arnold gives the name High Seriousness. All the great poets have shown this. Wordsworth shows it throughout his work. He never can show it too much. But presently in reading him we become wearied. We think it is by his sustained seriousness. But it is not. Seriousness of this kind never wearies. It is the quality which preserves Swift's work, which gives reality to Dante, which gives to Carlyle's work its great value, which is the best of M. Rolland, or Mr Masefield, or Ibsen. And of these we do not tire. We think we get tired of Wordsworth's seriousness, but what tires us is that the real seriousness sometimes shades off into false seriousness. The poet loses clearness of perspective. From seriousness over the real, he sometimes passes to solemnity over what is unimportant. The reader is justifiably bored. But the reader is not justified if he confuses the one thing, the fine rare thing, with the other. The true Florimel must not be punished because the false Florimel has appeared alongside of her.

Not only in this respect is a virtue accompanied by something that seems like it, but is really a defect, but also in others. Wordsworth and Coleridge both set out with great powers of writing. Coleridge let his lie unused, and the sinews of expression went stiff with him. Wordsworth used his. He practised self-expression almost before he knew what he wanted to say, and in the end he overworked his gift. He wrote too much. And his poetry (there is no denying it), when it is not of the best, can be curiously tedious and indistinctive. There is much of it that leaves no impression. It lacks character. Because of this, much beauty that his work actually does contain, to-day remains unexplored.

Also, it has been said that Wordsworth had to create the taste by which he was enjoyed*. It might equally be said that he created the taste by which he was destroyed. He succeeded in presenting a freshness of

* At the conclusion of his review of the course of English Poetry in the *Essay*, *Supplementary to the Preface* (of 1815) Wordsworth expresses the opinion "that every Author, as far as he is great and at the same time *original*, has had the task of *creating* the taste by which he is to be enjoyed:..."

vision, a newness of outlook. He created new interests. But some of these have now become so much part and parcel of most people's mentality that they have ceased to interest. These too have become hackneyed. Appreciation of the externals of Nature is now a commonplace.

These three things—his solemnity, his prolixity, and the fact that a good deal of what he says is no longer new to us—operate against enjoyment of the poetry. Two of these are the fault of the poet. The third is not. It is just one of the accompanying circumstances of his art. And neither is the poet to blame for one last thing which operates against a widespread appreciation of his poetry. It is that much of the message is not for all, and will never be for all. Wordsworth, like Milton, and like Blake, who anticipated him in some ways, is remote. Like Milton, he was remote, not in the sense that he held aloof from life, but in the sense that what interested him, and was most real to him, was not always what interested his fellow-men. When the men of his day were most of them writing on love or war, Milton was pondering in his heart "things unattempted yet in Prose or Rhime." Most of the poetry that appeals to the multitude is written on things that the multitude has experienced. Wordsworth and Milton, though both passionate, were passionate over the things that are only felt by the few. The average man can follow Wordsworth (although without excessive transport) when he writes of the Wye Valley. But when it comes to the story of his wooing by "un-

known modes of being," by the "huge and mighty
Forms" that were a trouble to his dreams—many
readers fall back in dismay or apathy. Wordsworth,
like Milton, would attempt no middle flight. He would
fain chant a great spousal verse. But the consum-
mation of his rapture is not such as all men understand.
The poet would

> ...arouse the sensual from their sleep
> Of Death, and win the vacant and the vain
> To noble raptures;

But alas, when he looks round, he finds that his
audience has taken advantage of his absorption to
slip away while his chant was going on.

And even when he touches on human things, it is
not, for the most part, on the "things done, that took
the eye and had the price" that he touches, nor are the
emotions he interprets the more obvious ones. It has
been said of him :* "...the passions he loved to depict
are not those that storm themselves out or rush to a
catastrophe, but those that hold the soul in a vice for
long years." And the passions that are apt to attract
the attention of the many are precisely those that storm
to a catastrophe. This again is not one of the faults of
the poet, but another of the circumstances of his art.

Yet even after admission has been made of the ex-
ternal circumstances that have obscured Wordsworth's
poetry, of the defects of the poet, and of the harshness
of some of the circumstances of his art, we are left with
the knowledge that Wordsworth's poetry enriches the

* A. C. Bradley, *Oxford Lectures on Poetry*, p. 121.

reader with the treasure of an inheritance no other poet could have given. Were everything that could contribute to obscure the lustre of the poetry magnified a hundredfold, it would not alter one whit the rare value of what Wordsworth has left for those who can see it. All those things that tend to obscure the value of Wordsworth's poetry are negative, and the quality of the poetry itself is positive. Therefore it is in no danger from the vicissitudes brought by time, or fashion, or taste, as poetry less absolute might be, for there is something in it that cannot die. It is worth considering wherein this precious inheritance consists, because such a consideration brings us up against the realities of the poetry to which Wordsworth gave his life.

For some readers, the greater part of this inheritance consists in the ethical motives of the verse, in the honour given in this verse to courage, fortitude, endurance, and in the penetrating analysis of states of suffering which the poetry gives. This sensitiveness to suffering, and interest in it, are shown in his poetry from the very beginning. They form the central interest of *The Female Vagrant*. His analysis arrests and interests, as in *The Borderers*, for example, where he contrasts the transitoriness of action with the permanence of suffering:

> Action is transitory—a step, a blow,
> The motion of a muscle—this way or that—
> 'Tis done, and in the after-vacancy
> We wonder at ourselves like men betrayed:
> Suffering is permanent, obscure and dark,
> And shares the nature of infinity.

We are interested in the healing he prescribes. It is that of the psalmist.

> And if there be whom broken ties
> Afflict, or injuries assail,
> Yon hazy ridges to their eyes
> Present a glorious scale,

Again, in 1819 he writes:

One who was suffering tumult in his soul
Yet failed to seek the sure relief of prayer,
Went forth—his course surrendering to the care
Of the fierce wind, while mid-day lightnings prowl
Insidiously, untimely thunders growl;
While trees, dim-seen, in frenzied numbers, tear
The lingering remnant of their yellow hair,
And shivering wolves, surprised with darkness, howl
As if the sun were not. He raised his eye
Soul-smitten; for, that instant did appear
Large space ('mid dreadful clouds) of purest sky,
An azure disc—shield of Tranquillity;
Invisible, unlooked-for, minister
Of providential goodness ever nigh!

The poet's prescription interests; there are moods in which it might help. But we know that we are not in the region of absolute truth. There are sorrows in which the hills do not help.

So—even in the midst of our appreciation, we find ourselves veering towards criticism of our poet:

> ...the Gods approve
> The depth, and not the tumult, of the soul;

says Protesilaus. But sometimes we feel that we get

neither the tumult nor the depth. We could do without
the tumult, but not without the depth.

It would be unjust to the reality which Wordsworth
gives us, however, to dally longer with the negatives
of criticism. A good test of the value of poetry is the
residue it leaves behind. Those who read many books
are struck by this or that in the reading. But much
passes. It is by what is left, as part of the reader's
mind, that enduring value must be estimated. The
legacy left by many writers in this way is strangely
slight. Wordsworth's influence never passes away.
He, no less than Coleridge, worked for the Permanent.
From this wealth we select for comment three gifts
which he left to those who have come near his spirit.
The first precious thing which Wordsworth has to give
is the record of experience which the confessional
poems give. In poetic character this varies from the
magnificent chanting of the *Immortality Ode* and *The
Prelude*—a chanting at times stormy and terrible
which has this in common with the poetry of Milton,
that it affects the mind like an incantation—to
the slender pipings in which Wordsworth tells of a
sweet and quiet communion. These poems narrate
a type of experience which other poets may have
felt, but which hitherto had not been put into words.
There are, as we have said, readers to whom this
kind of experience is uninteresting, but the manner
of its telling must appeal to anyone who cares for
poetry at all. And those who belong to the poet's
chosen audience "do make religion" of it. The

sense of a life shared with all created things, and
of union with these in the Infinite, is something
which interpenetrates the life of the lover of Wordsworth. It gives comfort and healing and the daily
bread whereon the spirit feeds.

No less precious is the second of the gifts of this poet,
to whom all the simple things of life are kin, and who
makes us kin with the wild things of the earth. This
gift is the realisation of the rhythm of life itself which
Wordsworth brings to us through his interpretation
of simple things and the lives of humble people. The
greatness of these poems and their purpose is on the
whole less well understood than the greatness of those
pieces in which Wordsworth gives expression to his own
moments of exaltation, but like those moments, they
have their roots in the poet's childhood, the period
which was of by far the most importance to his
poetry, and compared to which even the storms of the
French Revolution were but a momentary troubling
of the waters. These "low and wren-like warblings"
practically ceased after 1808. In them Wordsworth
gave of his best. The simple pieces have an even higher
truth than the magnificent ones. Wordsworth, early
in his career, realised the beauty of simple things, and
their value. He preached their healing power. He
sought the beauty of simplicity of expression to express
these simple things, and found it. He chose to be a
bard, keeping close to the people. It is difficult to
express just what Wordsworth put into these poems,
just the union of sensitiveness and delicacy and

imagination. They remind us that Wordsworth was very
much a simple man, and a dalesman. He travelled a
good deal : he took a keen interest in politics : he was
stirred by the fates of nations. But he was a boy bred
in the dales, and a man who chose the dales for his
enduring habitation. And he saw simple things in the
light of eternity. The strange sense of heartache that
comes from viewing the patience of a broken animal,
or the humility of an old peasant, or the tired curve
of an old man's back—that Wordsworth knew how to
express. The heartbreaking quality of the patience of
those who have little, stirred him to his depths. And
the poems in which he succeeds in expressing these
things seem symbolic of patience and permanence.
Their beauty is derived largely from the rare quality
of the poet's imagination, transfiguring and illuminating all it touches.

Some of these poems express the very poetry of
inarticulate humility. There is one passage in seven-
teenth century literature which sends us forward to
them, Bunyan's sweet singing of the uses of the Valley
of Humiliation "that nobody walks in but those that
love a pilgrim's life." There is one passage in the
literature of our own day that sends us back to them,
the passage (already mentioned in these essays) in the
first volume of *Jean-Christophe*, where Christophe sits
by the side of the river with his uncle Gottfried, and
Gottfried teaches the little boy to listen to the music
of the night*. Then he sings. Little Christophe had

* Romain Rolland, *Jean-Christophe*, i, pp. 185–9.

thought he was a musician, but anything like Gottfried's song he had never heard. It was like the spirit of the people put into words, full of inarticulate brooding over obscure memories, and troubles and joys. It was like unconscious music. And all the time Gottfried denied that it was music. He made no claim for it. It was just the speech of his soul. The whole passage is "haunting as music." This was just the kind of song, whose beauty and whose trouble and whose sugges-tions of the haunting of memory Wordsworth himself caught from his friend's description of the Highland reaper, and his own knowledge of what Gaelic song could be. This was the thrilling obscure message that the "plaintive numbers" carried to him. He under-stood it, no one better, and his poem expresses the trouble and the joy it brought him. It was his own song at its best, a song that is hardly music, but is full of the sweet and sad and shadowy suggestion of wide and solitary spaces and the obscure and heroic crea-tures who live out their destinies upon them. It haunts us too. It has a troubling quality, and its trouble is expressed in the lines:

> The Old Man's shape, and speech, all troubled me:
> In my mind's eye I seem'd to see him pace
> About the weary moors continually,

These simple poems show a deep sense of pity, but the sense of pity is always allied to optimism. Words-worth had a belief stronger than his being, that all things were significant and that consequently all was ultimately well—and he felt a necessity to expound

this belief. This optimism invests Wordsworth's
poetry with a healing quality for some readers. "I
have received more consolation from Mr Wordsworth's
poetry than from any sermons or works of devotion at
different times of my life,"* writes Sara Coleridge in
1846. Others are alienated by it, as it seems to them
to keep Wordsworth from confronting the belt of evil
and suffering that he could not explain. Such rot at
the heart of the universe as Shakespeare shows in
King Lear he will not contemplate. This is his limita-
tion. There are griefs for which the poetry of Wordsworth has no anodyne. Yet this is hardly a criticism.
Few of the poets can give any comfort when dealing
with this theme. There is not so much difference after
all between Shakespeare, who gave up wrestling with
it and turned at the end like so many of the poets to
Beauty for refuge, and Browning, who, in postulating
eternity as the solution of the problem, practically gave
up the defence of the world as it is, and Wordsworth
himself, who ignored the theme.

Even if we are vexed with Wordsworth for what
seems an evasion, we question whether it is legitimate
to demand of poetry that it deal with such matters.
There is just one refuge which poetry ought to give,
that of Beauty, and Beauty, the consoler, Wordsworth
gives in abundance.

Whereof this Beauty is composed, it is difficult to
say, for no poet has ever written with so few of the
sensuous accoutrements of poetry as Wordsworth. In

* *Memoir and Letters of Sara Coleridge*, II, p. 56.

this, as in other ways, he contrasts notably with Coleridge. He has not, like Coleridge, a book of enchanted words at his command—nor has he the colours of a witch's oils wherewith to tint his pictures, nor has he the gift of charmed sound. Surely no poet has ever worked with such economy of material. Yet Wordsworth achieved Beauty itself. To the end he never quite lost the power of conjuring up the shade of Helen.

His verse contains a multitude of those passages which inevitably become part of the reader's consciousness. This Beauty constitutes the remainder of the precious inheritance which Wordsworth passes on to those who love his poetry. There is in his work a multitude of these passages which take root in the memory and become part of the reader's mind. Especially notable is the number of fine single lines. It is a fair test for a poet to judge him by his highwater mark. Wordsworth does not fail under this test. Professor Elton seems to suggest this failure when he says: "With the masters of tragedy he does not come into comparison at all, either as a sage or as a poet." The first part of this may be conceded. Wordsworth was simple-minded. He would very likely have averted his eyes from the emotion of Medea or Phaedra, or the passion of De Flores; the unlegalised persistent devastating emotions were out of his ken. But in poetry surely he does not come short. He satisfies even the searching requirements of Arnold, giving as he does both the things which Arnold demands in his phrase

"criticism of life." His poetry at its best is both a
commentary on life and an illumination of it. Such
lines as

> The sounding cataract
> Haunted me like a passion:—

> At all times of the day and night
> This wretched Woman thither goes;
> And she is known to every star,
> And every wind that blows;—

> Thou art to me but as a wave
> Of the wild sea;—

and the long wash of Beauty closing perhaps the most
haunting verse of all his poetry:

> Breaking the silence of the seas
> Among the farthest Hebrides.—

can hold their own even alongside of

> in la sua volontade è nostre pace—

and

> Dark'n'd so, yet shon
> Above them all th' Arch Angel:

Poetry cannot be tested like a chain. If the
strength of a chain is according to the strength of its
weakest link, the strength of poetry is according to
the best of what it offers. And Wordsworth has much
of freshness, and fragrance, and understanding to give.

He would have been content to be judged in this
way, for if, like other men, he had his small vanities,
in the big things of poetry he was content to give or
take, to break or be broken. He had his light, and he
let it shine as he could, often on obscure places that

needed illumination, sometimes to throw the shadowy crags into dim splendour. As he tells us, the magnitude of the light is not the poet's affair. The poet must not waste himself in repining because his light cannot illumine the whole world. That is not his concern. The poet and the prophet alike are mouthpieces of a message greater than they. If they have but delivered their message, they have done their work, have given forth sweetness and have found peace.